CLASSIC ROCK CLIMBS IN
GREAT BRITAIN

Bill Birkett

The Oxford Illustrated Press

Photography by Bill Birkett

© Bill Birkett, 1986
Printed in England by J.H. Haynes & Co
Limited, Sparkford, Nr Yeovil, Somerset
The Oxford Illustrated Press, Sparkford,
Nr Yeovil, Somerset
ISBN 0 946609 30 6
Published in North America by Haynes
Publications Inc,
861 Lawrence Drive, Newbury Park,
California 91020
British Library Cataloguing in Publication
Data
Birkett, Bill
    Classic rock climbs of Great Britain.
    1. Rock climbing—Great Britain
    I. Title
    796.5'223'0941   GV199.44.G7
    ISBN 0-946609-30-6
Library of Congress Catalog Card Number
86-81826

CONTENTS

ACKNOWLEDGEMENTS

Many people helped and encouraged me in the preparation of this book, I would particularly like to thank the following:

John Adams, Jim Birkett, Chris Bonington, Tony Brindle, Sandra White (of Ballachulish), Paul Cornforth, Darrel Crilley, Chris Ann Crysdale, Frank Davies, Catherine Destivelle, Claudie Dunn, Ronnie Faux, Fiona Fraser (Tongadale Hotel), Mark Greenbank, Tony Greenbank, John Hargreaves, Steve Hubbard, Heather Johnson, Pat Littlejohn, John Lockley, Karen Long, Susan Lund, Dave Lyle, Louise McMahon, Pat McVae, Duncan Richards, Jon Rigby, Tony Sibley, Luke Steer, Denise Stratton, John Thorpe, Walt Unsworth, Tim Valley, Brenda Wilkinson, Iain (Wilf) Williamson and John White.

I would like to posthumously express by deep appreciation to both Bill Peascod, my very great friend, who always inspired and gave constant enthusiasm and Don Whillans, my hero and a legend in British climbing who simply said 'come down to Wales and we'll do some of them routes you want to photograph' and meant it.

For preparing and correcting the manuscript I would like to thank:

Julie Jones (typist), Susan Lund, Jon Rigby and Tom Waghorn.

For the use of published material I am indebted to:

Fell and Rock Climbing Club, Gollancz, Cicerone Press, Nelsonian Library.

Thanks are due also to Etsu Peascod and Tim Pavey for artwork, to Paul Renouf of PhotoScope for black and white printing.

To Big Jim and La'al Jim, father and son

INTRODUCTION

The order of the book is such that it begins with the most southerly tip of Britain and works its way northwards through five distinct areas. These are South-West England, Wales, Northern England, The Lake District, Scotland. Within each of these areas the climbs themselves are placed in ascending order of difficulty. If two, or more, separate routes are described in one feature then the easiest route dictates its position in the list. If, on the other hand the feature includes a combination of routes, where all the routes must be climbed to arrive at the top of the cliff, I have given the hardest route precedence in the list.

The length of the essays and the photographic content varies with the area. It can be seen that for routes in the south west some are illustrated less than those elsewhere; similarly the essays are shorter. This is not a comment on their quality as all the climbs chosen are excellent in their own particular way. It is simply that most of the routes in the south west are shorter—perhaps 70ft (21m) as opposed to 1000ft (305m) in Scotland—and because the size of the book was strictly limited, I felt it better to include more routes than expound at length on a lesser number.

Appropriately, the publication of this book, covering the essence of British rock climbing, coincides with the centenary of the event, on 27 June 1886, that first captured the imagination and excited the spirit of adventure in a very special group of people. It was the first ascent, solo, by W.P. Haskett-Smith, of the 70ft (21m) high striking thumb of rock in the English Lake District known as the Napes Needle.

This climb, despite its meagre proportions, was innovative and bold, the line being indisputedly aesthetic, and the widespread publicity it received, supplemented later by the superb photography of the Abraham brothers, captured the heart of an ever growing band of enthusiasts. They were, of course, rock climbers and the new sport (as opposed to mountaineering), was to be called rock climbing. Then, as now, it was decided that the pure physical action of climbing rock, as opposed to climbing specifically to reach a mountain's summit, was fun; its participation an end in itself.

Very quickly these early enthusiasts began to record and write up in detail both the routes they had ascended and the death-defying adventures they had enjoyed en-route. Today rock climbing, free climbing or sport climbing as it is variously called, is practised around the world. But in many ways it owes its origins, or at least has a close allegiance to, that spirited first ascent made by Haskett-Smith in 1886.

Since those early times, climbing, its standards, equipment and our approach to it, have changed considerably. This is good, for from each successive change, each wave of development, great and memorable climbs remain to be enjoyed. This book is a celebration of some of these climbs and of the people who shaped them.

Haskett-Smith is now acknowledged as the father of British rock climbing and he climbed throughout Britain (and abroad) recording in detail both the climbing areas and the climbs. Of his first ascent of Napes Needle he wrote:

'A deep crack offered a very obvious route . . . From the top of the crack there is no trouble to reach the shoulder, whence the final stage may be studied at ease. The summit is near, being as they say in Transatlantic cities "only two blocks away", but those same blocks are set one upon the other and the stability of the top one looks very doubtful . . . It seemed best to work up at the extreme right, where the corner projects a little, though the fact that you are hanging over the deep gap makes it rather a "nervy" proceeding. For anyone in a standing position at the corner it is easy to shuffle the feet sideways to the other end of the chink, where it is found that the side of the top block facing outwards is decidedly less vertical. Moreover, at the foot of this side there appeared to my great joy a protuberance which being covered with a lichenous growth, looked as if it might prove slippery, but was placed in the precise spot where it would be most useful in shortening the formidable stretch up to the top edge. Gently and cautiously transferring my weight, I reached up with my right hand and at last was able to feel the edge and prove it to be, not smooth and resounded as it might have been, but a flat and satisfactory grip.'

He also epitomised the rock climbing spirit. Well educated, first Eton and then Oxford, he shunned convention and chose to dress and conduct his life as he pleased—this rather rebellious, self expressive, devil-may-care attitude associated with the freedom of the hills has always since been an integral quality of the British rock climbing scene.

Haskett-Smith was described thus;

'Like many great men of strong personality Haskett Smith was full of little fads foibles and eccentricities . . . in later years his method of dress would be charitably described as careless. At dinners he always appeared in a well-known velvet jacket, quite dressy in itself, but somewhat spoiled by a shirt front lacking a stud and a tie resting anywhere but in the right place . . . such accidents caused him not the slightest embarrassment. On walks also his attire from hat to shoes was far from neat and he seemed to take a delight in making it as unsuitable as possible. There was . . . a long, square-cut, tail coat of thick check material with outside flap pockets . . . (which) appeared . . . only on the very hottest and most grilling of July or August days . . . On another day, in the Windsor neighbourhood he took us on a personally conducted tour over Eton College. The amazement apparent on the faces of the many Eton boys who were strolling about on the Sunday afternoon was highly amusing and I doubt very much they would have readily believed that the very shabbily and somewhat eccentrically dressed elderly man . . . was himself a very distinguished old Etonian.'

But, in many ways, it was really the next great personality on the scene that set the mould for much future development. O.G. Jones (he described himself as the 'Only' 'Genuine' Jones) was a brilliant and forceful rock climbing pioneer. Inspired to climb by a photograph of Napes Needle he wrote:

'I have a vivid recollection of walking down the Strand one wet spring afternoon in 1891, oppressed with the commonplace London streets and the flatness of the people and things in general, and crossing over by sheer force of habit to Spooners Photograph shop. In the centre of the window, and eclipsing to my perverted vision every other object around it, was a striking enlargement from the original half-plate of Dixon's Needle. I heard a by-stander at my elbow draw his friends attention to the figures in the picture with the remark "Scott! what fools." But that evening a copy of the Needle hung in my room; in a fortnight Easter had come round and I found myself on top of the Pinnacle.'

He pushed himself to the limit and sometimes beyond. The result was a leap in the standards of difficulty—up to Very Severe before the turn of the century. He outraged the establishment, trained for climbing and was strong enough, it is reputed, to have been able to do a one arm pull up—with a fellow climber crooked in his other arm. His climbs remain as more than ample testiment to his extraordinary powers. Unfortunately in the last year of the 19th century his luck ran out and he was pulled to his death in an Alpine accident.

His legacy was a book entitled *Rock Climbing in the English Lake District.*

Beautifully illustrated by the Abraham brothers it set the standard for all subsequent works. It is really from this point onwards that this book draws its material. The climbs selected are chosen for a variety of reasons (and there are so many more which should be included but cannot be) but many are hallmarks of both difficulty and quality for their particular period of climbing development. A few such examples being as follows:

Cioch Direct on the Island of Skye where in 1907 H. Harland and A. Abraham, sporting tweeds and nailed boots, trundled tons of gabbro blocks from the 1000ft (330m) face of Sron na Ciche to make their Severe climb. An epic of considerable proportions where the outcome was always in doubt and where they were constantly in danger of being crushed by the hugh flakes of detached gabbro that barred their way. True adventure in traditional style.

Central Buttress on Scafell where in 1914 S.W. Herford stood on the shoulders of G.S. Sansom to force the Great Flake—a climb that remains as one of the biggest single advances in rock climbing. The ghost of Herford still watches the efforts of many a struggling modern-day leader.

Overhanging Bastion on Castle Rock where in 1939 a young Lakeland lad and his two companions, Jim Birkett with C.R. Wilson and L. Muscroft, climbed the centre of the overhanging face and thought nothing of it. An unprotected lead that broke through a significant psychological barrier. Afterwards that which had previously seemed impossible became climbable.

Cenotaph Corner on Dinas Cromlech where in 1952 Joe Brown and Doug Belshaw climbed the perfect corner and created a climb that evocatively typifies the Brown era; possibly the most famous rock climb and most famous rock climber of all time.

Sloth on the Roaches where in the 1950s Don Whillans fearlessly jammed across the horizontal roof that presents the most striking challenge of the grit edge. He went on to become one of Britain's greatest mountaineers and a legend in his own lifetime.

Old Man of Stoer a sea stack off the north-west coast of Scotland where Dr. Tom Patey, with B. Robertson, B. Henderson and P. Nunn used two ladders tied together to cross the sea channel and reach the most enjoyable of all the sea stacks climbed by 'Dr. Stack'.

Footless Crow on Goat Crag where in 1974 Pete Livesy prepared and then free climbed into a new standard of difficulty—hopping from small hold to small hold unable to stop.

The variety of Britain's climbing is

outstanding and its roots are well represented in all three of the classified types: igneous, sedimentary and metamorphic. This is the main reason why individually our climbs are so remarkably different in character. Correspondingly the actual environment of the different locations could hardly be more diverse. There are climbs, described here, where you step from your car onto 300ft (90m) of vertical limestone, where you can walk many miles to high and lonely mountain cliffs of solid granite and those on which you first splash your feet in the sea.

In traditional spirit this book describes in words, photographs and diagrams some 62 of Britain's rock climbs. They may be extremely hard, or easier, but whatever their degree of difficulty they have a quality which is best described as classic. It is my own personal selection, restricted (naturally enough) to a printable number and by prevailing weather conditions during the time of preparation, but it is a fair representation of Britain's finest.

Classic Rock Climbs of Great Britain is both a guide to, and an appreciation of, these climbs. Firstly, it contains all the factual information required to locate the climb, decide if it is feasible under the prevailing weather conditions and then to actually climb the route and descend in safety. Secondly, there is an essay which in conjunction with my photographs, is an experience in words and vision of that climb (or climbs).

The guide portion of the information has been organised and is presented in such a manner as to facilitate climbing at a variety of grades (from moderate to E5) throughout the whole length of Britain. The descriptions of the climbs and the grades themselves are my own. Using the information provided, combined with sound judgement, it is possible to make the best of British weather throughout the four seasons of the year. And in traditional manner, because of the range of climbing grades, it is possible to organise your climbing in all but the very worst of conditions.

I am the son of a rock climber and have climbed, in Britain, for over 20 years. Indeed, I have walked amongst our hills for considerably longer than this. It's true to say that climbing and mountains are my life. The essays attached to each route relate not only the facts, the physical moves, possible protection placements, the history, but my own adventures, and capture the feeling and spirit of the individual route. There is no set formulae, I have simply written from the heart. (Although, I have striven to avoid describing the all about any particular climb. My intention being to whet the appetite only.)

Undoubtedly the essays, descriptions and my feelings for any particular climb, or area, have been shaped and influenced by those with whom I have had the good fortune to know and to climb. A number of these have made a considerable impact on British climbing development and are rightly recognised as some of the foremost pioneers of the sport. My father, Jim Birkett, of course, is one. He introduced me to the world of mountains, their flora and fauna, and showed me, as no one else could, the freedom of the hills.

His gifted and fluid movement on the steepest and most insecure ground has to be seen to be believed. He showed me how to belay, how to abseil and then, typically, left me to get on with it. Jim Birkett's climbs have been described as pure gold.

Another profound influence with whom I climbed many a fine climb, had many a laugh and shared a kindred spirit was Bill Peascod. His mastery of bold, delicate, climbing remained with him to the last. He died on Great Slab, when his heart failed, roped between Don Whillans and myself. It was a perfect climbers' death and he knew and suffered nothing. He left us his art and climbs as proof of his creativity and passion.

Don Whillans whose brief aquaintance made me realise that the man was actually bigger than the legend; was known universally for his hard and brilliant climbs. I found with him, sincere friendship. He was a man also of exceedingly sharp intellect and possessed the ability to assess a person's mettle in double quick time. The day after Bill's death we climbed a new route together – only because that's what we knew how to do best.

Of the more recent pioneers I suppose Pat Littlejohn, with whom I climbed in Derbyshire and Pete Livesey, with whom I've only ever exchanged insults (on the friendliest of terms of course), shape the material in this book. I remember Pat for his quiet nature off the crag and his explosive power whilst on it. A man with an outstanding record of development all over the south-west of England. Pete who advanced modern rock climbing with a series of incredibly hard first ascents and who is a superbly fit athlete, a top canoeist, caver and runner but, who, in the true traditions of rock climbing, with his straggly mat of hair and askew glasses, doesn't actually look fit enough to catch a bus.

Regarding the difficulty of the climbs, primarily I have chosen routes which I think merit classic status. These range from moderate to E5. On certain days some climbers will wish to climb hard routes. On other days, perhaps when the weather is not so clement, many will stay climbing and reduce the grade. Others will only climb Extreme, some only on mountain crags and yet others would prefer to do good 'Very Difficults'. So be it, climbers are strong individuals, but for the sake of equilibrium I have pitched my average at Very Severe and the majority of the climbs in this book are about that grade.

My philosophy is this: that rock climbing is many things to many different people on many different days. For me there is the pure thrill of climbing, the wonder of our superb natural environment, the joy of good companionship. Sometimes one of these takes precedent, sometimes all three go towards that unforgettable rock climbing day.

This is a book for the rock climber—in practice and in spirit. If within its pages you hear a little of the joy, solace, drama, peace and beauty of lonely wild places, pure physical involvement with rock and love for climbing that I have found—then it has whispered what I hoped it would.

Using This Book

The book is split geographically into five areas:
South-West England covering an area from Cornwall north through Devon and on to Cheddar (11 essays covering 16 climbs).
Wales including the South Pembroke sea cliffs, Anglesey sea cliffs, Snowdonia and North Wales area (8 essays covering 13 climbs).
Northern England Peak District, Yorkshire and Lancashire (6 essays covering 10 climbs).
English Lake District all major areas (10 essays covering 13 climbs).
Scotland from the Cairngorms in the east, to Glencoe in the west and north to the Island of Skye and the north-west mainland coast (8 essays covering 10 climbs).

For each climb there is an introductory list of information which is mainly self-explanatory but the following comments should be noted.

Grading of Climbs

The dual subjective and numerical/adjectival British system of grading rock climbs has been adopted. The grades apportioned are my own and may be at slight variance with information elsewhere, but should prove consistent throughout the different areas.

Generally within the text only climbs of Very Severe stature and above have been given a technical grading, e.g. Great Slab—600ft (183m), Very Severe (Overall Grade) (4c, 4a, 4b, –, –) (Technical Grade for each pitch).

Below is a table showing the Overall Grade, which is an impression grade based on length and seriousness (difficulty in placing protection) and the range of technical difficulty that may be reasonably expected in this overall grade.

Used Together		
British Overall Grade		British Technical Grade
Moderate		1a
Difficult		2a
Very Difficult		2b
Severe (Mild)		2c, 3a
Severe		3a, 3b
Severe (Hard)		3b, 3c
Very Severe (Mild)		4a, 4b
Very Severe		4b, 4c
Very Severe (Hard)		4c, 5a
Extremely severe	E1	5a, 5b
	E2	5b, 5c
	E3	5c, 6a
	E4	6a, 6b
	E5	6a, 6b
	E6	6b, 6c
	E7	6c, 7a

British Overall Grade and
Corresponding Technical (Pitch) Grading

The following is a table comparing the British system of technical grading with some of the most popular grading systems used elsewhere in the world. The table utilises my own experiences and those of many others. However, this is not an absolute guarantee of accuracy and it is intended as a guide only.

Table Comparing International Grading Systems

Britain	France	UIAA	USA	Australia
4a	4 + V	V	5,6	15
4b	5 –	V +	5,7	16
4c	5	VI–	5,8	17
5a	5 +	VI	5,9	18
5b	6a	VI +	5,10a	19
		VII–	5,10b	20
5c	6b	VII	5,10c	21
			5,10d	
		VII +	5,11a	22
6a	6c	VIII–	5,11b	23
		VIII	5,11c	24
6b	7a	VIII +	5,11d	25
6c	7b	IX	5,12a	26
				27
		IX	5,12b	28
7a	7c		5,12c	
		IX +	5,12d	
	8a	X–	5,13a	

9

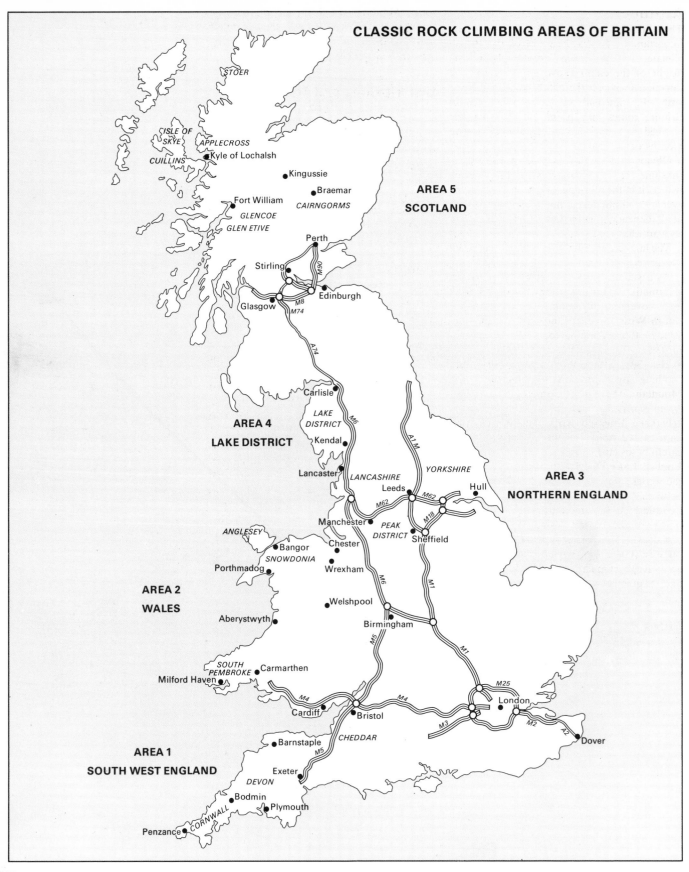

CLASSIC ROCK CLIMBING AREAS OF BRITAIN

STOER

ISLE OF SKYE
APPLECROSS
CUILLINS
● Kyle of Lochalsh

● Kingussie

AREA 5
SCOTLAND

● Braemar
● Fort William
CAIRNGORMS
GLENCOE
GLEN ETIVE

● Perth

● Stirling
M90

● Edinburgh

● Glasgow
M8
M74

A74

● Carlisle

LAKE DISTRICT

AREA 4
LAKE DISTRICT

● Kendal
M6

A1M

● Lancaster
LANCASHIRE
YORKSHIRE

● Hull

AREA 3
NORTHERN ENGLAND

● Leeds
M62
M62
M18

● Manchester
PEAK DISTRICT
● Sheffield

ANGLESEY
● Bangor
● Chester
SNOWDONIA

● Porthmadog

● Wrexham
M6
M1

AREA 2
WALES

● Welshpool

● Aberystwyth

● Birmingham

M5

SOUTH PEMBROKE
● Carmarthen
● Milford Haven

M4
M25

● Cardiff
M4
M4
● London

● Bristol
M3
M2
A2
● Dover

CHEDDAR

AREA 1
SOUTH WEST ENGLAND

● Barnstaple
M5

● Exeter
DEVON

● Bodmin
● Plymouth
CORNWALL
● Penzance

Attitude

This information is simple but extremely important to get the best out of the British climate. By giving sensible thought to the height of the climb above sea level and the direction in which the climb faces, combined with the seasonal climatical divisions in Britain, routes may be selected that can be climbed at some time throughout all twelve months of the year.

Obviously a south-facing climb will get the sunshine throughout the day; one facing east will get it in the morning; one facing west in the evening and one facing north may never see it at all (depending on the time of year) or receive its warmth.

The higher the cliff above sea level the colder the air temperature.

As a general guide the following climatical information is worth knowing for the different areas covered in the book:

South-West Mildest and hottest area of Britain. Rock climbing for twelve months of the year.

Wales Sea cliffs and low-lying crags—rock climbing for twelve months of the year. Mountain areas: rock climbing usually between April and October.

Northern England Rock climbing for perhaps twelve months of the year if the crag is carefully selected.

English Lake District A mountain area and the wettest region of England. Rock climbing between April and October.

Scotland A mountain area and the most northerly and coldest region of Britain. The east coast (Cairngorms) is generally drier than the west (Glencoe) though it is also the coldest area. Rock climbing generally between May and September. (Beware of midges; carry repellent.)

Tides

On sea cliffs it is extremely important to study the tide times and cycles. Tides can rise by some 30ft (9m) (low to high) and this fluctuates throughout the year. Check them carefully (information from local coast guard) and beware of freak waves at all times.

Descriptions and Descents

All information (UNLESS stated to the contrary) is given looking at the climb (or crag). Therefore *right* and *left* are relative to the climber *facing in*. This is true for both the climbing descriptions and the descents—because it is usual to work out your descent route from the ground, prior to climbing.

Beware also of rock falls, etc., that may subsequently change the character of the route from that described here.

Dangers

Despite modern protection, or what anyone may say to the contrary, rock climbing is dangerous. I have lost too many good friends to know otherwise.

Anything less than total concentration, and awareness of the dangers, throughout the climbing day can lead to tragedy.

This book assumes a thorough understanding of, and sound practical ability with, all techniques and equipment currently in use in British rock climbing.

Beware of the sea, always, on sea cliffs. Sunshine and calm do not remove its danger.

Beware of rapidly changing weather, particularly in the mountains. A high, long mountain route, in Wales, the Lakes or especially Scotland, is always a serious proposition irrespective of technical difficulty. Always carry adequate clothing, a warm summer's day in the Scottish Highlands can rapidly deteriorate and even turn to snow.

Photography

All the photography (unless stated otherwise) is my own. It is 35mm and mainly consists of colour transparencies.

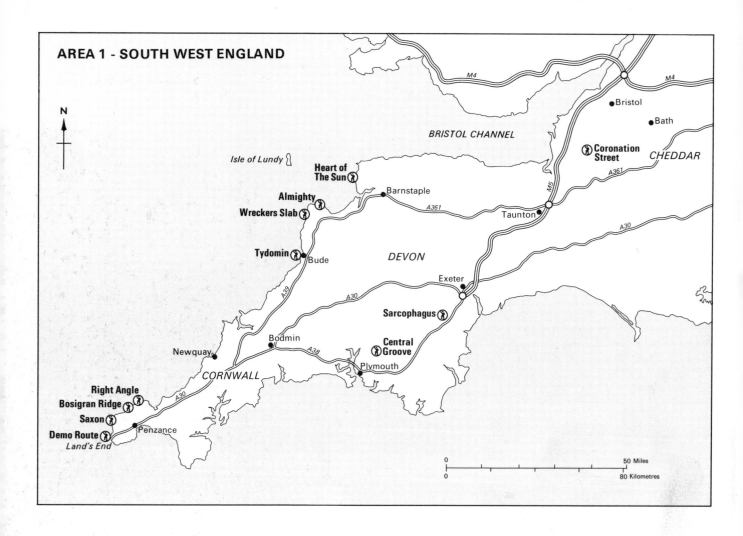

AREA 1 - SOUTH WEST ENGLAND

N

BRISTOL CHANNEL

• Bristol

• Bath

Ⓧ **Coronation Street**

CHEDDAR

Isle of Lundy

Heart of The Sun Ⓧ

M4

M4

M5

A361

Almighty Ⓧ

Wreckers Slab Ⓧ

• Barnstaple

A361

Taunton •Ⓞ

DEVON

A30

Tydomin Ⓧ

•Bude

A39

A30

Exeter •Ⓞ

Sarcophagus Ⓧ

Newquay •

Bodmin •

A38

Central Groove Ⓧ

• Plymouth

CORNWALL

A30

Right Angle Ⓧ

Bosigran Ridge Ⓧ

Saxon Ⓧ

Demo Route Ⓧ

•Penzance

Land's End

0   50 Miles

0   80 Kilometres

SOUTH-WEST ENGLAND: Demo Route and Corner Climb

DEMO ROUTE: 80ft (24m). Hard Severe.
First Ascent: Royal Marines *circa* 1950s.
CORNER CLIMB: 70ft (21m). Difficult.
First Ascent: Unknown, *circa* 1940s.
Location: Sennen Cove, north coast of West Cornwall.
Map Ref: 347263 (Sheet 203).
Guidebooks: *South-West Climbs* by Pat Littlejohn. *Cornwall – West Penwith* by Pete O'Sullivan.
Attitude: Faces west, situated just above sea.
Rock: The best Cornwall granite.
Tides: Accessible at all tides but beware of rough seas.
Access: From the car park at the very end of the road follow path to top of the cliff—about 5 minutes' walk. At low tide it is possible to follow round the beach to the foot of the climbs, but the slabs can be horrendously slippery due to the seaweed and care is required. To the south an easy scramble leads down to below the cliffs and one can then gain the terrace below the climbs. Along the left end of the terrace an orange wall stands cleanly at right angles to the cliff. The centre of the wall is taken by Demo Route.

Demo Route – Summary

Start 30ft (9m) left of the corner at the bottom of a flake.

1. 80ft (24m), (4b). Up the flake to gain a niche. Continue awkwardly to a good horizontal break. Move left until it is possible to pull over the overhang into a short corner with a slab on its left, which leads to the top.

Corner Climb – Summary

Climb the corner on brilliant holds and jams to the top.

Demo Route and Corner Climb – Description

Sennen Cove is a traditional Cornish fishing village with a wide panorama across a bay where the aquamarine waves drive in from the Atlantic. Sennen is attractive quite apart from its climbing, noted for its sunsets, its surfing and its occasional shark. The cliff, although none too high, consists of impeccable Cornish granite and most probably there isn't a loose or suspect hold on the whole cliff. It is beautiful rock from black to orange-red to marble-white in colour, solid and rough to hold.

Sennen is a fun place with a good variety of climbs all of which dry rapidly, although climbing cannot be guaranteed when the seas are high and rough.

Demo is *the* classic route of its grade in the area. It's not easy and gradually increases in difficulty to a fitting and memorable finale. The start up flakes leads to a comfortable niche, sporting an awkward crack. Alterna-

DEMO ROUTE: 80ft (24m). Hard Severe.

DEMO ROUTE, CORNER CLIMB

crux

climber in the niche

Demo Route

Corner Climb

belay point

tively this may be quitted in favour of elegant moves up the right wall. Both lead to a good horizontal break and possible belay. A traverse left leads to holds above the overlap. The position feels extreme, the rock bulges considerable and confidence is required to commit oneself to undercut jams and secretive rugosities. Commitment, once made, is repaid in full and the top reached with joint senses of relief and disappointment. Relief that the crux has been climbed and disappointment because the route is over.

Corner Route gives a fine direct way up the cliff involving a number of different techniques on beautiful granite jugs. Two excellent climbs of their grade which characterise the host of other steep routes which are to be enjoyed here.

Left: **John White on Corner Climb; brilliant holds and jams take him to the top.**

Wilf Williamson on typical Cornish granite.

SOUTH-WEST ENGLAND: Bosigran Ridge (Commando Ridge)

Bosigran Ridge drawn by my late, great friend, Bill Peascod.

COMMANDO RIDGE: 700ft (213m). Very Difficult.
First Ascent: A. W. Andrews and Miss Andrews, 1902.
Location: Bosigran, West Penwith, Cornwall, south-west England.
Map Ref: 416369.
Guidebooks: *Cornwall—West Penwith* by Pete O'Sullivan. *South-West Climbs* by Pat Littlejohn.
Attitude: Sea cliff, faces west.
Rock: Impeccable granite.
Access: Takes the distinct granite ridge opposite Bosigran main cliff on the south-west edge of Porthmoina Cove. Approach from the mine ruins down a well-worn path leading to the coast. When the ridge can be seen break left, following path until ridge can be crossed via a

distinct notch. Climb down the back of the notch until it is possible to scramble down. At low/medium tide start beneath the foot of ridge. If seas prevent this cross slabs and start a little higher.

Bosigran Ridge (Commando Ridge) – Summary

Start by moving round to a platform and then gain the wall on the left. Continue up via a ledge and the cracked wall until the broad top of the first pinnacle can be reached. Up the chimney to the apex of the ridge and follow this where possible. Eventually the notch is reached and a descent can be made to the Commando plaque, rucksack and sandwiches.

Bosigran Ridge (Commando Ridge) – Description

Cornwall, its manners and customs, its descendant peoples, its moors and seascapes, is an intriguing land. Out of season, beyond the garish facades, tourist traps and stultifying second-home communities, there is a real Cornwall, wonderfully wild, fresh and secretive. This is a world in its own right, virtually an independent country tagged on to mainstream Britain.

The rock climber is privileged, as an outsider, for he is privy to these unspoilt places and free to savour the real character of the area. We can still scour the rocks for minerals, descend the smugglers' steps and be alone with the inhospitable, wonderfully savage sea. It is a status that should be guarded zealously.

A. W. Andrews and his sister first ascended Bosigran Ridge around the turn of the century and in many respects it remains the masterpiece of Cornish sea-cliff exploration. Andrews was the originator and mentor of British sea-cliff climbing and his enthusiastic activities spanned half a century. Remarkably he realised its attractions many years before it reached the celebrated and popular position it now occupies in rock climbing. He wrote:

'The sea forms unique climbing surroundings and the weather is good. There are no long walks to crags, and there is no necessity to be miserable in order to feel that the sport is being suitably indulged.'

All very true and the following verse, written by Andrews, goes a little further into capturing the essence and excitement of this often perilous branch of rock climbing:

'A cliff we could not climb and on our right
Nothing but sea, America and night.
When time and tide were flowing much too fast
And each escape seemed trickier than the last.'

Left: **Wilf Williamson starting Bosigran Ridge.**

Right: **Wilf Williamson straddling Bosigran Ridge.**

This was real Cornwall as the summer tourist will never see it; wild and deserted.

But suddenly it was fine and weak rays of sun lit the droplets on the window. We threw on our boots and wind-proofs; it was time to visit the cliffs.

That sea was wild, breaking and crashing so high that suds of foam blew across the top of the rocks, and the blueness of it made it exclusively Cornwall. The rock had dried within half an hour and what rock. Perfect granite with friction, texture and beautiful square-cut holds and jugs that made you want to climb on it for ever. We gained the ridge across some steep slabs and walls, being unable to start at the base. Even so that sea threatened and terrified. Exposure was immediate and remained so throughout the length of the route.

The climbing is exciting, on a pure sharp fin of granite all the way, and I can't remember a single move on the whole ridge that I didn't enjoy. Positions, too, are amazing and the variety surprising, with possibly the hardest moves crossing a little wall on the Bosigran side of the ridge early in the ascent.

Bosigran Ridge is more than a climb, it's an adventure. It left me with the feeling that I had at last tasted something unique to Cornwall, something that had real character. I returned to the Count House positively wanting to meet the ghost and congratulate her.

Pinnacles of granite on Commando Ridge.

From the Count House window (Climbers' Club hut next to the deserted mine), warmed by a roaring fire, I watched the April clouds, black and angry, race across the sky. I listened contentedly to the screaming moan of the wind, sea and rain with the certainty that I could laze undisturbed for the rest of the day.

climber

belay point

SOUTH-WEST ENGLAND: Right Angle

RIGHT ANGLE: 245ft (75 m). Hard Severe.
First Ascent: I.M. Peters, J. Bember, 1966.
Location: Gurnard's Head, West Penwith, north coast of Cornwall.
Map Ref: 432388 (Sheet 203).
Guidebooks: *South-West Climbs* by Pat Littlejohn. *Cornwall – West Penwith* by Pete O'Sullivan.
Attitude: Faces south-west.
Tides: Not affected by tides.
Rock: Metamorphosed greenstone—hard and with sound holds.
Access: From the Gurnard's Head Hotel follow the sign-posted path via a number of intriguing granite steps. Continue along the headland until a gully gives access to the first pitch. The cliff rises directly out of the sea, and the climb takes a line some way above this and is therefore not affected. (10 minutes.)

Right Angle – Summary

Takes the distinct black corner rising above the sea.

1. 55ft (17m), (4a). Traverse right, down a few feet crossing a groove to a good ledge.

2. 60ft (18m), (4b). Traverse again to the top of a vertical crack. Descend down this to its base, move right a few feet and back up to a distinct ledge and peg belays.

3. 130ft. (40m), (4a). Move up the wall towards the corner, surmount the overlap and continue up the corner to the top.

Right Angle – Description

Gurnard's Head sticks out very distinctively into the Atlantic. At first sight the rock appears disappointing; jet black and rotten-

John White on the first pitch of **RIGHT ANGLE:** 245ft (75m). Hard Severe.

Above left: **John White starting the second pitch of Right Angle.**

Above right: **In the corner above the sea cave.**

looking. Yet although not granite and therefore slippier in the wet, it is surprisingly very good. On arrival, Right Angle lies invisibly beneath you and it's worthwhile dumping your gear and walking until you get a reasonable view of the climb. It's a remarkably powerful looking little route.

Rightly named, this climb takes the powerful looking black corner at the back of the inlet. For its grade the climb is impressive, tackling very steep rock above a live sea, a sea which alternately sucks and crashes, deep water which is never still. Once embarked upon there can be no downwards escape and the seriousness of the situation adds to the climb's special charisma.

Both holds and runners are good, which is fortunate as the climbing becomes immediately meaningful. It owes its length, almost 250ft (76m) to the fact that it climbs in and down to

its *raison d'etre*—the challenging corner cutting clearly upwards from the measureless black cavern.

The descent of the vertical crack on the second pitch, although well protected by wires, is reasonably·demanding. Keep cool and when all else fails try the left wall where hidden jugs lurk smilingly. The belay ledge and its in-situ, sea-spattered pitons, offers only cold comfort for very near now the cavern echoes and amplifies the sounds of the sea, and above the main challenge patiently awaits your attention.

Right Angle occupies a position usually reserved for routes of much greater technical severity. It places the climber in the world of commitment, but at a reasonable standard, and the rewards are accordingly greater. And don't worry about that last pitch, it's really quite reasonable.

Above: **John White in the top corner of Central Groove.**

Below: **The bottom corner of Central Groove.**

SOUTH-WEST ENGLAND: Central Groove

CENTRAL GROOVE: 180 (55m). Hard Severe (4b, 4b).

First Ascent: J. Cortland-Simpson and party, 1949.

Location: Devil's Rock, The Dewerstone near Shaugh Prior, South Devon, about 8 miles (13 km) north-east of Plymouth.

Map Ref: 538638 (Sheet 201).

Guidebook: *South-West Climbs* by Pat Littlejohn.

Attitude: Lies in a sheltered valley facing south.

Rock: Rough granite.

Access: On the south of Shaugh Bridge there is parking by some abandoned granite masonry kilns. From here cross over the wooden footbridge and continue along the path above the river (north bank). After about a quarter of a mile or so, passing a few smallish rocks, the Devil's Rock is reached—lying just above the river (10 minutes).

Central Groove – Summary

Start below the large open groove.

1. 100ft (30m), (4b). Climb the crack in the wall to gain the ledge below the corner. Continue directly up, utilising the cracks in the right wall for both progress and excellent nut protection (Friends 2–3). When the overhang is reached move right, ascending across the wall to gain the right arete. Move up onto the detached block to stance and nut belays.

2. 80ft (24m), (4b). Up onto easy ramp leading rightwards to the final slanting corner.

Central Groove – Description

An interesting chat on black magic and the supernatural with the landlady of the 'Skylark' the previous evening had set the mood for our visit to the Devil's Rock. A night spent on the open moor in March, followed by an early

CENTRAL GROOVE

Central Groove

belay point

thoughts of the occult evaporated and my eye was immediately drawn to the line of the crag—a 100ft (30m) open vertical corner.

Central Groove is a fine natural line on immaculate granite, tackling the most obvious challenge of Devil's Rock. The climbing is as good as it looks with a variety of moves on unrelentingly steep ground. The crag, sheltered from the elements, can be warm and pleasant to climb upon throughout the year. Due to the rough nature of the rock it is still a reasonable proposition to climb even when wet.

Awkward moves from the ground lead to a ledge and the corner proper. This is ascended with the assistance of two hand sinking cracks on the right side and frequent foot-ledges on your left. Although steep, it never pushes you unduly even when the overhang is reached and you make exhilarating and surprising moves out to the right, across the wall, leading to a good stance.

Thereafter a broad ramp leads easily to what constitutes the crux of the climb if wet. A well-defined corner offers a finger crack and layaway holds that deliver you, hopefully, to the top of a rather splendid route.

CENTRAL GROOVE: 180ft (55m).
Hard Severe (4b, 4b).

morning start through leafless trees, black and dripping moss, compounded the feeling of mild panic that hovered in a dark corner of my imagination.

As if by magic, on arrival at the rock, the sun broke through the grey sky to reveal a crag of most beautiful fine-grained granite. A revelation, the area became transformed,

SOUTH-WEST ENGLAND: Wrecker's Slab

WRECKER'S SLAB: 430ft (131m). Hard
Severe.
First Ascent: Tom Patey, J.H. Deacon, K.M.
Lawder, 1959.
Location: Cornakey Cliff on the Culm coast a
few miles north of Bude.
Map Ref: 204165 (Sheet 190).
Guidebook: *South-West Climbs* by Pat
Littlejohn.
Attitude: Faces south and remains warm and

sheltered even in mid-winter.
Tides: Easy access low to half tide.
Rock: Metamorphosed shale.
Access: Ask permission and park at Cornakey
farm, follow the farm track until the coastal path
is reached (15 minutes). Immediately below you
lies the huge cliff of Cornakey. Gain the foot of
the climb by an easy scramble down the
northern edge of the cliff and at low to half tides
walk across the beach. If the tide is in it is

John White at the top of
Wrecker's Slab.

23

Above left and right: **The first and second pitches on Wrecker's Slab.**

possible to traverse the slabs at about severe standard, although rough seas would make this impossible.

Wrecker's Slab – Summary

Takes the longest and most obvious slab in the centre of the cliff. The rock is predictably dubious and care is always required. There are a number of fixed protection pitons which appear sound and additionally a friend 2 protects the crux and a Friend 2–3 gives a secure second belay.

1. 140ft (43m). Start on the left of the slab and up and left until a groove leads past a protection peg and to peg and nut belays.

2. 150ft (46m). Continue up the groove to the overlap (Friend 2), which is the crux, and move up and left to surmount it. Continue upwards following the best holds until you reach a ledge below a cracked pinnacle (Friend

in crack for belay).

3. 140ft (43m). Jam up the crack and continue up the left edge of the slab to the top.

Wrecker's Slab – Description

Wrecker's Slab is blatantly huge; a 400-ft (122-m) slab tilting up the side of an even larger cliff. Its setting, on the rugged and deserted Devon coast, is also very special. Rising from a beach of stone footballs it basks in sunshine and warms the heart of even the coldest winter day. Although the rock is metamorphosed shale, and intrinsically unsound to pull upon, it is predictable in its nature and runs to block-type holds and cracks. Once an allowance is made for the general rock quality it genuinely warrants a Hard Severe rating. Climbing quality is high and the exposure immense.

I was drawn to the route, down from the distant north, because it was a Tom Patey route; the charisma of Patey, the character of his explorations, I find compulsive. There was no disappointment; the route lives up to his reputation. It's an adventure, a classic, and a great climb.

There are a number of pitons en-route and these are reassuringly sound. After the first 120ft (37m) or so the first peg is reached in the groove on the left of the main slab and a few feet higher another peg and the belay. Above, it looks imposing with the groove being overlapped by the slab above. Additionally grass chokes the groove and the climbing looks decidedly worrying. Surprisingly it's not too bad and the overlap is surmounted by moving left onto clean rock, the grassy groove being quitted entirely for good holds leading to the edge of the slab. Follow these up to a good ledge and belays. Below, the boulders on the beach change rapidly to pebbles and then into marbles as you progress upwards. When we climbed, the big cliff atmosphere was heightened by a nesting kestrel flitting nervously over the huge slabs and intervening vertical walls and by a black raven which glided silently and powerfully beneath our feet.

Classic jamming lasts for only a few feet until excellent holds, and sunshine, elevate you all too quickly to the top and the end of a notable climb.

WRECKERS SLAB

jam crack

crux

climber

belay point

WRECKER'S SLAB: 430ft (131m). Hard Severe.

SOUTH-WEST ENGLAND: Sarcophagus

John White at the crux of Sarcophagus.

SARCOPHAGUS: 110ft (33m). Mild Very Severe (4b).
First Ascent: T.W. Patey, 1960.
Location: Chudleigh Rocks, Near Exeter, south Devon.
Map Ref: 864786 (Sheet 202).
Guidebooks: *South-West Climbs* by Pat Littlejohn.

Attitude: Faces south.
Rock: Hard limestone.
Access: Chudleigh village is only nine miles south-west of Exeter, just off the A38. At the western end of the village a narrow road leads past a police station to parking by an iron kissing gate on the right (just before a large gated yard). Through the gate and follow the

SARCOPHAGUS

top section obscured

T. PAVEY
111285

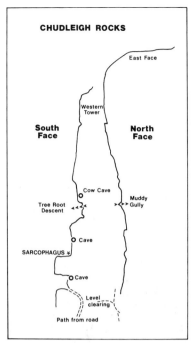

CHUDLEIGH ROCKS

East Face

Western Tower

South Face

North Face

Cow Cave

Tree Root Descent

Muddy Gully

Cave

SARCOPHAGUS *

Cave

Level clearing

Path from road

Above: **Chudleigh Rocks layout.**
Left: **SARCOPHAGUS: 110ft (33m). Mild Very Severe (4b).**

path for 200 yards (180m) or so until the end of the rocks are visible. The south face lies down to the left and the big corner of Sarcophagus a couple of hundred feet along this (5 minutes).

Sarcophagus – Summary

Start in the corner.

1. 110ft (33m), (4b). Up the cracks to a cave ledge. Move out and up using the chimney to reach a further block overhang. Break out left across a polished slab until moves up enable a nose on the right to be utilised. Pass a ledge (possible belay) and continue up the corner line to a stout tree belay.

Sarcophagus – Description

Chudleigh Rocks could never, truthfully, be described as good-looking. They rise inelegantly from the jungle of foliage and trees

27

below, through a series of broken walls and ledges liberally spattered with vegetation. Yet there are some good, if not obvious, little climbs and one which immediately strikes you as being outstanding.

Sarcophagus is the white clean corner which leans out, in a series of block overhangs, above you. Tom Patey named it so and it takes little imagination to realise why. When you are up there, in the corner, the clean faced blocks entomb you both physically and mentally. It's very easy to feel trapped.

It was a very bold first lead (or was it solo?) for the problem looks considerably harder than its actual grade of Mild Very Severe. Also those great jutting blocks of limestone do look potentially insecure. But there are no worries with respect to loose rock for it is sound and remarkably hard limestone. So hard in fact it has taken a high polish, a factor which added to its difficulties.

Space walking is a much clichéd expression, but it is wholly apt for this tremendous little route. Starting is awkward, insecure but only vertical. After 20ft (6m) from the comfort of a good ledge the overhanging rock above can be leisurely perused. It isn't too bad, especially if one makes use of everything that is offered; you can jam your body in the chimney, feet on either wall and securely grip the blocks with your hands. That is until you move leftwards; quitting the chimney is balancy but the difficulty soon relents.

On the way back I stopped and read the two notices I'd ignored on the approach; one was a warning about bats, the other that climbing, on Chudleigh Rocks, was dangerous. Both were justified and seemed, somehow, complementary.

TYDOMIN, CRIMTYPHON, CARAVANSERAI

Caravanserai

Tydomin

descent rake

peg

Crimtyphon

start
obscured

fin of rock

belay point

SOUTH-WEST ENGLAND: Tydomin, Crimtyphon and Caravanserai

TYDOMIN: 90ft (27 m). Very Severe (4c).
First Ascent: K. Darbyshire and D. Garner, 1974.
CRIMTYPHON: 100ft (30m). E1 (5b).
First Ascent: K. Darbyshire and D. Garner, 1974.
CARAVANSERAI: 110ft (33m). Hard Very Severe (5a).
First Ascent: K. Darbyshire and A. Clarke, 1975.
Location: Compass Point, Bude, Culm coast, North Cornwall.
Map Ref: 099064 (Sheet 190).
Guidebook: *South-West Climbs* by Pat Littlejohn.
Attitude: Faces south.
Tides: Only affected at highest tides.

Rock: Metamorphosed shale—sound and hard, the best on the Culm coast.
Access: From Bude take the narrow road that follows the canal on the south side of Bude Haven. Park before the end and continue along to a kissing gate. Through this until one can ascend leftwards to the Compass Tower (4 minutes). Directly below a 100-ft (30-m) high sharp fin of rock runs out to sea. The climbs lie on the left (south) side of this and are reached by an easy rake some way along the ridge.

Tydomin – Summary

On the left of the first big corner, left of the descent rake, is a slabby wall. Tydomin climbs it.

TYDOMIN: 90ft (27m). Very Severe (4c). **CRIMTYPHON:** 100ft (30m). E1 (5b). **CARAVANSERAI:** 110ft (33m). Hard Very Severe (5a).

29

Crimtyphon – Summary

Takes the steep slab right of the descent rake, starting right of the sea caves.

1. 100 ft. (5b) This pitch links the obvious pockets and mainly relies on in situ peg protection (seemingly sound in 1985). Up to the large pocket and either go up to a smaller pocket and then step down and left, or move directly leftwards to an in situ peg. Past this to a further large pocket (peg). Move left and up to the small pocket (peg) and continue up more or less directly via the weakness (further peg runner).

Caravanserai – Summary

Right again the most obvious corner groove is reached via a horizontal ramp 15ft (5m) above the shore.

1. 110ft (33m), (5a). Gain the ramp, move right, and follow the corner to the top (good Friend protection). The top left is a shaley scramble and it is advisable to place a good runner before commencing.

Tydomin, Crimtyphon and Caravanserai – Description

Compass Point sticks out from the Compass Tower at Bude like the steep ribbon of a plastic razor—a single bedding plane, deserted by its brother rocks. The south face of this resulting knife-edge ridge gives some really excellent off-vertical climbing. This location for a quick session on the rocks could hardly be more bizarre, for Bude is an extremely popular seaside resort. If you like ice-cream or fancy a climbing break with the family—it's the place to go.

Climbing could hardly be more accessible and even amenable to a winter day's activity. It's no more than a few minutes walk and remains sunny and sheltered. Undoubtedly the rock is the best on the Culm coast and generally gives adequate and reliable holds.

I have included these three climbs not only because they all give superb climbing within their 100ft (30m) height but because each one typifies the grade. To have three climbs, so doing, lying virtually side by side must be a unique occurrence.

Tydomin (VS) offers steep rock resembling the scaly skin of some prehistoric beast. There are plenty of holds but none of them large and the 4c standard is maintained throughout its 90ft (27m). Protection is scarce and a cool, collected approach is essential.

The next one over—Crimtyphon (E1) gives steep and balancy wall climbing with good but well spread in-situ peg protection. Its 'climbing wall' type climbing links the pockets which can

John White climbing solo near the top of Tydomin.

1. 90ft (27m), (4c). Climb just right of the arete, there is an in-situ peg runner where the arete indents, thereafter, as the slab unfolds, one tends slightly rightwards.

be picked out as the only features on this otherwise blank-looking sheet of rock. Each pocket brings a hold and a welcome rest, from whence the next series of moves can be assessed. In its own way it's a technical masterpiece which keeps you thinking right to the top.

Caravanserai (HVS) is different again. Probably the steepest of the trilogy, it features chunky jams, solid laybacks, large footholds and the 'all placed' protection is regular and dependable. This is good as one tends to race up the climb before suddenly realising its steepness and your position of vulnerability. A good nut should be placed before one quits the crack for the shaley exit to stake belays.

All in all these are three distinctive climbs in their own right; together they brighten even the gloomiest winter afternoon or enhance the variety of a family holiday.

Mid-way on Crimtyphon.

SAXON: **160ft (49m)**. Hard Very
Severe (5a, 5a).

SOUTH-WEST ENGLAND: Saxon

SAXON: 160ft (49m). Hard Very Severe (5a, 5a).
First Ascent: P.R. Littlejohn, S.B. Jones, 1974.

Location: Carn Kenidjack near St. Just, north coast of West Cornwall.
Map Ref: 354 326 (Sheet 203).

Guidebooks: *South West Climbs* by Pat Littlejohn. *Cornwall – West Penwith* by Pete O'Sullivan.

Attitude: Faces south-west in a tiny sheltered zone.

Tides: Access at all tides.

Rocks: Hard Killas slate featuring reliable sharp holds.

Access: From the steep sided valley below St. Just on the Botallack side, follow a narrow lane on the seaward side, this rapidly deteriorates, but continue on until some way up the hill a track breaks off left. Follow this to its end in a small quarry. Directly below, grass leads to a steepening ridge which gives access to a narrow zone. Saxon takes a line up the fine-looking back wall (5 minutes).

Saxon – Summary

Start left of the enormous boulder which lies on the right-hand side of the zawn.

1. 25ft (8m), (5a). Gain the ramp, the hardest move on the climb, and move left to its end and a nut belay.

2. 135ft (41m), (5a). Continue up to a niche up the wall above following the line of least resistance until a very obvious horizontal crack (good runners) is reached. Move right a few feet then follow the line of holds directly to the top of the crag.

Saxon – Description

This is a really pleasant climb on sharp, reliable holds. It starts from a tiny zawn, with views of headlands and rocky islands washed by the copper-blue Cornish sea, and moves rapidly into the insular world of technical difficulty and verticality. The runners are

Above left: **John White starting the second pitch on Saxon.**
Above right: **High on the second pitch, the horizontal crack.**

spaced, but good, and the climbing constantly absorbing with no worries about loose rock. This is how I prefer to climb.

After 150ft (46m) you are still climbing and the moves are as hard as anything else on the route. It is here, on the vertical head wall, above a horizontal crack laced with good runners, where you can most appreciate the satisfying nature of the climb. A lot of rock, and many intricate moves separate you from your second down below.

To the second, the wall between is a blur of steepness, but to you it is a vivid memory of sharp finger-holds, crystal pockets and quartz-vein footholds. Both, however, can be suitably impressed for the position looks tenuous and it is only fine judgement that separates you.

The area surrounding is a maze of mines and industrial archaeology—you have passed through one of the most extensively mined locations in Cornwall. Old tin workings and their proximity and relationship with the sea add an extra dimension to this steep little route. As the waves crash in from the Atlantic, and the sinking sun turns the sea silver, keep an eye open for Sammy seal who often swims by, stopping to watch curiously man's return to these now quiet cliffs.

Above the ledge belay of Saxon.

SOUTH-WEST ENGLAND: The Almighty and Sacre Coeur (Sacred Heart)

THE ALMIGHTY: 250ft (76m). Hard Very Severe (4b, 4b, 4c).
First Ascent: S.B. Jones, P.R. Littlejohn and K. Goodman, 1971.
SACRE COEUR: 120ft (37m). Extremely Severe (E2, 5b/c).
First Ascent: P.R. Littlejohn and H. Clarke, 1977.
Location: Blackchurch on the Culm coast near Clovelly, North Devon.
Map Ref: 299266 (Sheet 190).
Guidebooks: *South-West Climbs* by Pat Littlejohn.
Attitude: North facing.
Tides: Sacre Coeur is affected by the tides but

The Almighty can be reached except at unduly high tide.
Rock: Metamorphosed shale.
Access: Approach via coastal path from Brownsham Farm (Map ref: 286259), 20 minutes. The Almighty lies on the far left of the striking main crag, starting at an obvious crack line leading to a large pinnacle. Sacre Coeur climbs the seaward slab of the impressive triangular stack.

The Almighty – Summary
(Continuously loose and serious).
1. 100ft (30m), (4b). Up the cracks until a

Above left: **John White at the first crack on The Almighty.**
Above right: **The last few feet of The Almighty.**

35

right, past a protection piton, to make further moves round the rib to small stance and belay (Friend 3).

3. 90ft (27m), (4c). Traverse right into a shallow groove, move down slightly and move right again. Continue straight up on to the slab moving left, as soon as possible, and follow the edge (in situ peg protection) on better holds to the top and thank your lucky stars you're still alive.

Sacre Coeur – Summary

Good rock, perfect protection, brilliant climbing—a complete contrast to The Almighty. Climb the obvious crack system in the slab.

1. 120ft (37m), (5b/c). Climb to a slot at 20ft (6m) move left delicately into the main crack which is followed until moves right, near the top, lead to a hairline crack and the summit.

The Almighty and Sacre Coeur – Description

The approach from Brownsham Farm couldn't be more pleasant. In March the primroses and wild daffodils coloured our descent into mixed deciduous woods and so to a quaint little Devon bay. The cliff is different, imposing, loose and always dark and foreboding, yet it has an unexplainable, fatal, attraction. The Almighty is perhaps the most frightening and serious sea cliff climb I've ever done. The Hard Very Severe grade is a mere attempt to reconcile simple technicality with dramatic exposure and the loose nature of the rock. Perhaps the snow lying above and below the crag and the cold north wind influenced my judgement unduly—but I don't think so. The introductory crack rapidly indicates what is to follow. When the pinnacle is reached and the top looped with rope it becomes very obvious it's as potentially lethal as the rest of the cliff, and when you heave onto the protection-less rib from its summit, you suddenly become aware of the full meaning of the word commitment. Eventually a stance is reached, but it only serves to accentuate the exposure and inescapability. Moves right again lead across a crumbling groove and then to the foot of an expanding slab. Above looks diabolical with vertical grass on your right and a precarious-looking slab to the left. But take heart, step daintily above the void, and move up and left to better holds, an in situ protection piton, and the top. Always dark, facing north, it never sees the sun and in the cold light of reason you may ask why I have included it. Yes it's serious and loose and all I can say is do it then you'll know. You will only do it once, but you'll know.

Above: **Mid-way on Sacre Coeur.**
Far right: **Committment above the pinnacle on second pitch of The Almighty.**

broken rib leads to a large pinnacle, use its top to belay but stance a few feet lower.

2. 60ft (18m), (4b). Step from the top of the pinnacle to gain steep rib. Follow until forced

Sacre Coeur is a completely contrasting experience to The Almighty. A superb climb which is a balance of delicate footwork and slim finger pulls. Perfect rock, brilliant protection and a unique setting make this climb a must for the technically proficient.

The common denominator between these two vastly different experiences is the name Pat Littlejohn; probably the single most influential figure in the history of South-West climbing. Three things stand out with Littlejohn, as I discovered when once climbing with him; first his modesty, second his calm, reasoned approach, and third the immense power of the man. This balance of strength, physical and mental, goes some way to explain his incredible legacy of exploration, including the contrasting Almighty and Sacre Coeur.

He and his partners climbed The Almighty on sight—that is without previously attempting or inspecting the route—and naturally enough, it took them a full day, Pat later described it to me in typical understatement as 'A big adventure'! The traverse right, onto the final slab which I had found totally intimidating, then consisted of collapsing, muddy ledges—all of which have now vanished. Pat admitted that even he had found this section 'horrendous'. At that time the final slab was totally unknown and Pat had no piton runners. It's still bold but then, it must have rated as one of the most courageous leads of the time—a journey into the unknown on steep, vegetated rock of highly dubious quality with no belays worth bothering about. Right at the top of this huge cliff and with no means of safe retreat (you need belays for that!), 'The Almighty' does seem a rather apt name.

Subsequently, when preparing his Guide *South-West Climbs,* Pat abseiled down The Almighty and cleaned up the route, placing a number of pitons for security, to make it safer and more attractive. He said to me

'I thought if the loose was cleaned off and the belays were made safe people would enjoy climbing it. In fact it would be a true middle grade classic Very Severe. But I think it's deteriorated slightly again, maybe it's HVS now!'

One sunny day found Littlejohn stuck in Exeter without transport, trying to reach Keith Darbyshire (later to be tragically killed doing what he most relished—pioneering a new route) who was climbing at Blackchurch. Pat searched desperately for transport, until finally borrowing his grandfather's moped, he sped to Blackchurch at full speed—25 mph. After a three-hour journey he was so cold it took him half-an-hour to walk. When he eventually arrived at the cliff he found Darbyshire

half-way up what was to become Sacre Coeur, but Darbyshire, however, backed off and Pat was rewarded with the lead—sacred heart indeed.

These two routes should be on everyone's list of climbs to do in the south west. Together they give the complete spectrum; on their own they remain magnificent.

THE ALMIGHTY: 250ft (76m).
Hard Very Severe (4b, 4b, 4c).
SACRE COEUR: 120ft (37m).
Extremely Severe (E2, 5b/c).

THE ALMIGHTY

Friend belays

crux

large detatched pinnacle

The Almighty   climber

belay point

SOUTH-WEST ENGLAND: Coronation Street

CORONATION STREET: 400ft (122m)
Extremely Severe, E1 (5b).
First Ascent: C.J.S. Bonington, J. Cleare, A. Greenbank, 1965.
Location: High Rock, Cheddar Gorge, Somerset, on the B3371 Cheddar/Bath road.
Map Ref: 472542 Sheet 183.
Guidebooks: *Cheddar* by Richard Broomhead. *South West Climbs* by Pat Littlejohn.
Attitude: Faces north-north-west and can be cold, although dries very quickly.
Rock: Limestone.
Restrictions: Because of the proximity of the road and tourists, both immediately below, climbing is restricted to the winter months, and is allowed between October and May, exclusive of Easter week.
Access: High Rock is the most obvious and largest wall shooting up from the right-hand side of the gorge (as you drive up). Immediately below there is a lay-by but wise climbers park, out of range, on the other side of the gorge (10 seconds).

Coronation Street – Summary

Start in the distinct corner.

1, 2. 160ft (44m), (4b). Up the corner to belay.

3. 70ft (21m), (5a). Up and leftwards, over the overlap to gain the groove. Continue directly until the chimney gives access to a good stance and belays.

4. 50ft (15m), (5a). Up the crack to the overhang and hand traverse left, over the 'shield', to a hanging stance.

5. 80ft (24m), (5b). Move right and follow the corner and crack until a step right to a small stance, peg and Friend belay.

6. 50ft (15m), (5a). Move right a few feet then up the Wall, passing a sapling to easy ground and the top.

Coronation Street – Description

I'm not really a Cheddar fan. It's always seemed rather cold, damp, vegetated and loose when I've climbed there (always in mid winter)—feelings proved not unfounded when

CORONATION STREET: 400ft (122m). Extremely Severe, E1 (5b).

CORONATION STREET

hanging belay

The Shield

○ belay point

Coronation Street

Rick Graham pulled a hold and crushed a vertebra, but that's another story.

Coronation Street is exceptional. Now solid and vegetation free, it takes a courageous line up the 400-ft (122-m) vertical face of High Rock. You step straight from your car onto the climb, from tranquility to high tension. It's undoubtedly one of the greatest limestone climbs of its grade in Britain.

The first 170 ft (58m) or so give comforting climbing up the well-defined corner, surrounded on either side by luxuriant ivy. When it was first climbed this must have been the pits, but now the vegetation doesn't touch the climbing and it's quite acceptable. Suddenly you break left, aiming for the good-looking groove which gives access through the overlaps to the crack line above. The climbing begins immediately with bold bridging enabling lay-away holds above the first overlap to be reached. Then you're out there, nothing below your feet, a whole lot of very, very steep rock above, and inside you buzz because you know you're on a great route.

The groove steepens and overhangs, with real exposure thumping your heart, to the belay. It's a good feeling.

Everyone will recognise the next section, the 'Shield' pitch. After the vertical crack a hand traverse leads wildly, via the distinct white flake, to a hanging stance. An old foot sling still hangs there, alarming the senses to imaginary terrors, but the hand holds above it are wonderful.

After this, the groove pitch would be superb on the ground on its own. With 300ft (91m) of space below you it's spellbinding. The hardest moves lie here, but security is high too. At its top you step right and can take another stance. Why not enjoy the position? Finally a short wall is climbed and even this lonely last few feet stand out and satisfy the senses.

What a marvellous climb. First climbed, of course, by two Lakes' lads—Bonners and Tony Greenbank with John Cleare taking the photographs. Yes I know one of them slipped slightly into Himalayan-type stuff, but nobody's perfect and the other remains essentially pure. Second time round it was done for TV (and why not), by Bonners and Mike Thompson. But Tony had the last word—'Coronation Street,' he called it, 'Hey man, wow, brill-ee-aant'.

Above: **John White climbing the lonely last few feet of Coronation Street.**
Left: **Approaching the Shield.**

41

SOUTH-WEST ENGLAND: Heart of The Sun

Wilf Williamson at the crux of the second pitch on Heart of The Sun.

HEART OF THE SUN: 330ft (100m).
Extremely Severe E2 (5a, 5b, 5c).
First Ascent: Tony Willmott and Mike Spring, Autumn 1969.
First Free Ascent: Arnis Strapcans and Chris King, June 1976.
Location: Slab Cove, Baggy Point, North Devon.
Map Ref: 419406 (Sheet 180).
Guidebooks: *South-West Climbs* by Pat Littlejohn, *North Devon Guide*.
Attitude: Sea cliff, facing south west.

Tides: Only high spring tides affect the bottom of the climb.
Rock: Metamorphosed shale.
Access: From the National Trust car park at the end of the public road at Croyde Bay, a track gives a pleasant 20 minutes walk to overlook Long Rock Slab down on the left and Slab Cove over on the right (the highest cliff). Drop down a small path and contour round, crossing rock fall and scree debris, to reach the cove (30 minutes).

Heart of the Sun – Summary

Start just left of the main slab at the base of a groove, where a thin crack tails gently upwards.

1. 45ft (14m), (5a). Gain the crack and up to a ledge in the groove.

2. 120ft (37m), (5b). Descend down rightwards and traverse until the crack can be reached in the middle of the slab. Up this to belay on fixed gear.

3. 165ft (50m), (5c). Continue up the crack until the corner can be gained. Follow this almost to the top where moves left lead to the edge of the slab and easier climbing to the top. (It may well be wise to fix a belay—extra rope from warning sign—before climb is started.)

Heart of the Sun – Description

The cliff is deceptively high, around 250ft (76m), and the first thing that hits you is the great big yellow slab with a huge bedding plane, running up the middle. The second thing you notice is the huge pile of rock debris that spreads down and into the cove.

Driving through Croyde I had been suitably impressed by the large number of attractively bronzed surfers and also by a local newspaper headline 'Baggy Point Falls Down'. Well, if we were too late, we could always surf.

Circumnavigating the little approach path was intimidating with huge blocks and lesser avalanche debris spewed above, below and across. It wasn't the actual cliff that had slipped but the head of the cove to its right.

As my partner (Wilf Williamson) set out up the first pitch I kept looking over my shoulder, just waiting for the rest of the cliff to crash down upon us. Sure enough, a high pitched whoosh followed by three sharp cracks marked what I instantly imagined to be a further rockfall. But nothing happened until I heard the same noises again. This time I picked out the bright stars of the coast guard's flare. We were to find out later that a fishing boat had lost its rudder and was consequently adrift. The flares were part of the rescue procedure, fired from a Land-Rover that had been driven to the top of the cliff.

The first pitch (now) starts left of the main slab and immediately gives interesting climbing. The next long pitch lingers fondly in the memory—a descending traverse right into the centre of the slab requiring a confident approach. (No protection for 35ft, 11m.) When the hairline crack is reached protection can be found. Harder climbing begins and finger holds and balance get you up. Before the belay is reached (fixed gear) the bedding plane shudders into a vertical bulge. Peg protection

The first pitch on Heart of The Sun.

gives some security but moves are strenuous and technical.

Another very big pitch follows, 165ft (50m)

HEART OF THE SUN: 330ft (100m). Extremely Severe E2 (5a, 5b, 5c).

HEART OF THE SUN

belay
well back

crux

serious
traverse

belay point

of rope won't get you to a belay, and gives the hardest moves. Finger jamming can be well protected (Friends) and leads to the corner which is a little loose and a little grassy. Continue straight up and over an overlap until near the top. Moves left lead to easy ground, the welcome heather and no belay. I had to begin climbing as Wilf crawled, on hands and knees to maximise the resistance if I fell, to a notice-post some little distance away.

Certainly extreme, Heart of the Sun is no eliminate but a superb and challenging line up the most obvious feature of the cliff. Available to everyone leading E2, Heart of the Sun represents the best of Devon sea cliff climbing. I felt it gave, like a Thomas Hardy novel, an honest, rich and often disturbing perspective of our England. Brilliant.

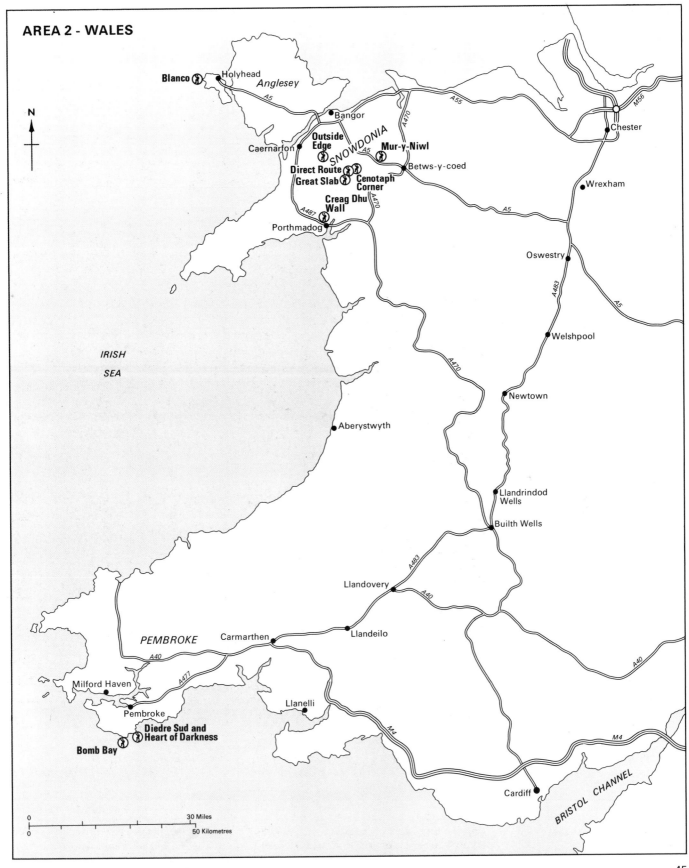

AREA 2 - WALES

N

Blanco 🧗 • Holyhead   *Anglesey*

A5

• Bangor

Outside Edge 🧗   *SNOWDONIA*   **Mur-y-Niwl** 🧗

Caernarfon •   *A5*

Direct Route 🧗   • Betws-y-coed

Great Slab 🧗   **Cenotaph Corner** 🧗

Creag Dhu Wall 🧗

A487

Porthmadog •   *A470*

A55

Chester ○

• Wrexham

• Oswestry

A483

• Welshpool

A5

A470

• Newtown

IRISH SEA

• Aberystwyth

• Llandrindod Wells

• Builth Wells

A483

• Llandovery

A40

PEMBROKE   Carmarthen •   • Llandeilo

A40   *A40*

A477

Milford Haven •

• Llanelli

Pembroke •

🧗🧗 **Diedre Sud and Heart of Darkness**

Bomb Bay 🧗

M4

M4   *BRISTOL CHANNEL*

Cardiff •

0 ————— 30 Miles
0 ————— 50 Kilometres

WALES: Outside Edge Route

Cwm Silyn.

OUTSIDE EDGE ROUTE: 400ft (122m). Very Difficult.
First Ascent: J. M. Edwards, C. H. S. R. Palmer, 1931.
Location: Craig Yr Ogof above Cwm Silyn, North Wales, Snowdonia National Park (near Caernarvon).
Map Ref: 517501.
Guidebook: *Snowdonia Rock Climbs* by Paul Williams.
Attitude: Faces south west.

Altitude: 1500ft (456m).
Rock: Rhyolite, good flake holds.
Access: From Llallyfni follow the road to Tan-yr-Allt until a turn right at a right-angled junction, can be made (after the second house on the left) up a narrow but surfaced road. After a farm (park here) this turns into a grass track. Follow this past the lakes into the bottom of the Cwm, then straight up the scree to the crag (45 minutes).

Outside Edge Route – Summary

Start about 25ft (8m) right of the left edge of the slabby wall, below a sizeable partly-detached flake block.

1. 75ft (23m). Up a groove to the block. Traverse across it to the left and up the steep wall to a shallow cave-like recess.

2. 65ft + 20ft (20m + 6m). Follow the flat-topped spikes up and leftwards, making a rising traverse to gain a groove at the arete. Straight up to ledge and belays. (The Ordinary Route—Difficult—comes in from the right at this point.) Best to continue for a further 20ft (6m) to gain Sunset Ledge.

3. 40ft (12m). From the left end of this (the ordinary route leaves via an obvious cleft at the mid point) move left across a groove into a second groove. Up this and step left to another large ledge. (Flake belay high up.)

4. 80ft (24m). Gain the obvious flake crack and up to a groove and continue through the overlap at the top until a belay ledge is reached.

5. 120ft (36m). The ridge becomes broken but follow it to a final interesting wall and then a few pinnacles to the top.

Descent: Follow the Great Stone Shoot towards the Right of the Amphitheatre.

Outside Edge Route – Description

Cwm Silyn is a delightfully quiet and charming amphitheatre of rock crowning twin copper-blue lakes which twinkle, seductively, below. The climb Outside Edge takes a bold and logical line up the splendid large buttress of rock, Craig Yr Ogof. Surprisingly, considering the gentleness of the approach, the climb has real Welsh mountain quality with the crags

Below left: **Darrel Crilley below the detached block on the first pitch of Outside Edge Route.**
Below right: **Past the layback crack of the fourth pitch.**

OUTSIDE EDGE ROUTE: 400ft (122m). Very Difficult.

OUTSIDE EDGE ROUTE

route obscured round corner

O belay point

of Myngdd Mawr over to the north, the volcano-like cones of the Lleyn Peninsula (Bwlch Mawr, Gurn Gooh and Gurn Ddu) behind, and the hillside below unfolding green fields to the sea and the Island of Anglesey. On a clear day the vista extends across Anglesey to the final bump of land, Holyhead mountain, then the sea and across this, shimmering on the horizon, the emerald hills of Ireland.

The position is one of space and depth, yet the Cwm retains a private subtlety, a quality sadly missing on the more popular Snowdonia Crags. I found Outside Edge to be one of the most enjoyable mountain climbs of its standard in Britain; a delight of the aforementioned qualities and also of good spiky rock and rapid movement. A route with a sense of purpose, a beginning, an end and form between. I wonder, as I write this, just what Menlove Edwards thought of it; perhaps a little too straightforward, too predictable, to be ranked highly in his estimation. There again, perhaps not.

The initial moves up a shallow corner are threatened by a huge block which appears to be stuck on to the rock merely by faith. When you reach it you realise that this, indeed, is the case. On the first ascent it must have required careful judgement and a degree of courage to commit oneself to the next series of moves along the top of the block. It still does in fact.

Quite awkward moves up lead to a shallow cave-like recess and a line of square-topped flakes leading boldly across the steep wall to the promise of a groove on the very outside edge of the wall. The situation here is spectacular.

I think without over-doing things I should expand on this theme, and paint a more detailed picture of the leader's situation. Edwards liked to be evocative and hated purely mechanical description:

'You can read it, the dry print, but only with headache' . . .
'The description is a tiny, narrow spotlight moving in a single line . . . the rocks might be any rocks, and the conformation of the cliff and climb might be any conformation, might be in mid-air, for the spotlight sheds no rays aside . . .

Well this position really deserves justice, it isn't just any position, another move, another route—a mundane experience. It's bold and imaginative, with lots of space below and unknown rocks above. It's a pity, in some respects, that we know the grade, have the knowledge that the moves across this wall lead to good holds and a sound groove. Imagine the first ascent, a great sweep of slabs over to the right, towering upwards for 300ft (91m) and below just space. For as you move right you attain a position on the very edge of a great perched buttress of rock. Here, all that's beneath is hundreds of feet of space and then a hillside which falls rapidly to the twin lakes many more hundreds of feet below.

The rock is clean on the edge; there aren't ledges to break the verticality or vegetation to lessen the perfection, or add an extra dimension, depending on your point of view. Afterwards, the climb maintains its interest, technically even gets harder near the end, when one enters a wide flake crack, but that upward flake traverse is, at least psychologically, the crux.

No whirlpool or 'do or die' solo on vegetated rocks, but I would like to think the Outside Edge had something special even for the great explorer, Menlove.

On the edge, second pitch.

WALES: Diedre Sud and Heart of Darkness

Across the bay to Mowing Word.

DIEDRE SUD: 140ft (43m). Hard Severe.
First Ascent: Colin Mortlock, S. Williams, 31st May 1967.
HEART OF DARKNESS: 190ft (60m). Hard Very Severe (4c with New Morning finish—5a).
First Ascent: Jim Perrin, J. Greenland, 13th August 1971.
Location: West Face of Mowing Word, South Pembrokeshire, Wales.
Map Ref: 992943.

(Both climbs are restricted from 1st March to 31st July, during the nesting season, when no climbing is allowed. This is a joint agreement negotiated between the BMC and the Nature Conservancy and should be strictly complied with.)
Guidebook: *Pembroke* by Jon de Montjoye and Mike Harber, published by the Climbers' Club, 1981.
Attitude: Sea cliff, faces west.

Rock: Limestone.

Access: Both climbs are situated on the 140ft (43m) high headland that is the West Face of Mowing Word; only separated horizontally by 200ft (61m) or less. Diedre Sud is the, full height, corner and Heart of Darkness traverses above the largest sea cave to the right of this. Each climb can be reached easily by abseil (take care with locating Heart of Darkness—if in doubt go further out to sea and then traverse back along ledges), making them climbable at most tides, but the 'classic' zawn approach is recommended for the ascent of Diedre Sud.

The climbs lie approximately 30 minutes' walk from either Broad Haven (to the west) or Stackpole Quay (to the east) car parks. The zawn approach may be utilised for two hours either side of low tide. West of Mowing Word is a noticeable inlet—Raming Hole (OS ref: 987944)—and starting near this a terrace leads down to two ring pegs and a 25ft (8m) drop, which can be done hand over hand, but is best abseiled (free at the bottom). Continue down the rock shelf through a sea cave, across the bay and, if the tide is high, through another sea cave to the foot of the big corner of Diedre Sud. Spectacular scenery and a real adventure.

Diedre Sud – Summary

1. 70ft (21m). (3c) Corner to belay ledge.
2. 70ft (21m). (4a) Corner until moves left at top overhang.

Heart of Darkness – Summary

Starts on the ledge right of the sea cave. If abseil is taken directly to this point you descend over a substantial roof. On the left, just below the base of the ledge, is an in-situ peg and nut belay. Here a semi-hanging stance can be taken with excellent views of the pitch to be climbed.

1. 100ft (33m), (4c). Up the edge of the pillar (right-hand pillar of the sea cave) to gain the hand traverse line leftwards. Follow this into and out of the corner until a stance on the edge can be taken.

2. 90ft (27m), (5a). The climb originally went left to Diedre Sud but it is more challenging to continue up the vertical flake crack directly above. Climb this (New Morning finish). Alternatively a slim groove over to the left (Razorbill—4c) also provides an excellent, but easier finish.

Diedre Sud and Heart of Darkness – Description

A wet wild day, with Christmas a few days hence, and the Abraham Club (an unofficial, loose-knit group of Lakeland climbers) were in truly 'fouguing' spirit. Diedre Sud, with the classic sea approach, seemed an ideal choice

and Broad Haven's serene beauty was instantly transformed as ten outsize feet ripped at her white-orange body. With no winners, and no losers, the rowdy contingent forayed on. A steep descent, frighteningly so, into a likely-looking bay, the wrong bay, did little to slow the pace. Up, and eventually past the Raming

Jon Rigby topping out of Diedre Sud.

DIEDRE SUD AND HEART OF DARKNESS

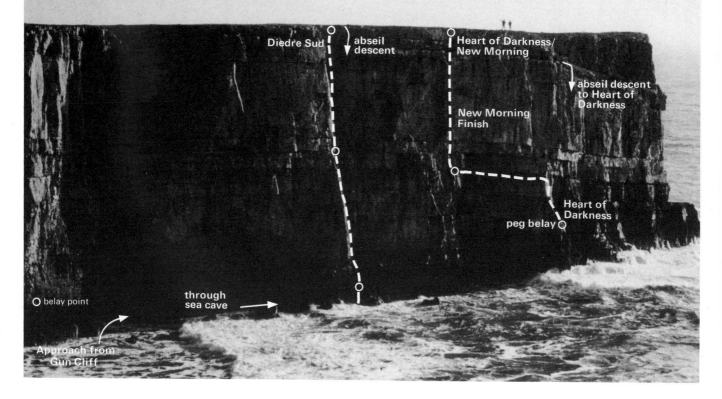

Diedre Sud / abseil descent / Heart of Darkness/ New Morning / abseil descent to Heart of Darkness / New Morning Finish / Heart of Darkness / peg belay / belay point / through sea cave / Approach from Gun Cliff

Top: **DIEDRE SUD: 140ft (43m).
Hard Severe. HEART OF
DARKNESS: 190ft (60m). Hard
Very Severe, (4c with New
Morning Finish – 5a).**
Above: **Wilf Williamson starting
Heart of Darkness.**

Hole, the correct descent located, the team continued with increasing enthusiasm as the quarry came into sight.

Hand over hand down the rock step (not recommended), led to an intoxicating world of caves, rock pillars, crashing waves, mirror-calm sand and there, up front, 140ft (43m) of verticality and the classic right-angle of our objective. Wilf Williamson got lashed by the sea so he was tied on for more, and Jon Rigby as well because he had the expedition sac to carry. Corny (Paul Cornforth) and I ran out up the corner belaying half way on the only ledge. Seconds rushed behind to escape the clawing sea. Up again, my wellies smearing effectively through the damp, lay-backing and bridging until more technical moves led to the left side of the overhang and then to the top. Solid climbing and all plumb vertical. We hooted and hollered back through the winds still managing a few shots of the storm-smote coastline. George and Ashley (Abraham) would have enjoyed it too.

Seas were still high and wild the day we decided to do Heart of Darkness. This time we started from Stackpole Quay and our pace and poise were more refined. It was lonely and beautiful. Pembroke should not be called 'Little England beyond Wales', for it is unique. The abseil was exciting, the rock wet and the eventually-found belay all-revealing.

The route climbs up the right side of a black sea cave, then traverses spectacularly between the abyss below and great overhangs above. Waves and the din of the sea, pounding close below you, mix with space, position and wet rock to provide a little fear to pump the adrenalin. The holds are generous, the best resembling turtle heads stuck in the numerous horizontal bands that lead across the void into the corner and out again, to safety. This pitch is good Hard Very Severe and above, the crack looks very, very steep. It's a tremendous climb and we voted it the best Christmas Day out ever.

CREAGH DHU WALL

crux
The Pinnacle

Creagh Dhu
Wall

belay point

WALES: Creagh Dhu Wall

CREAGH DHU WALL: 170ft (52m). Hard Severe (3c, 4a, 4a).
First Ascent: J. Cunningham, W. Smith, P. Vaughan, 12th July 1951.
Location: Craig Y Castell, Tremadog, Wales.
Map Ref: 557403.
Guidebooks: *Tremadog* by Leigh McGinley, *Snowdonia Rock Climbs* by Paul Williams, *Rock Climbing in Wales* by Ron James.
Attitude: Faces south west. Altitude: 400ft (131m).
Rock: Superbly crystalline volcanic dolerite (good friction, good holds).
Access: The crag lies five minutes' drive from Tremadog Cafe; just past the junction of the A4085 and A498 a lane leads to a school. Park thoughtfully and walk past the school until a hole in the wall leads over a muddy field to a scree and crag (15 minutes).

Creagh Dhu Wall – Summary

Lying centrally the line follows a groove initially, until exiting right and then back left gains the blunt nose which is followed to the top. Take the corner right of the overhangs starting from a little tree above a flat block.

1. 60ft (18m) (3c). From the tree go up until at the top one can traverse right across the slab to reach a crack. This leads to ledge and tree.

2. 80ft (24m), (4a). Back left to the edge and make a difficult move up and then straight up to a good ledge.

3. 30ft (9m), (4a). Up and left to gain, precariously, a sloping niche. Usually move left then up to finish.

CREAGH DHU WALL: 170ft (52m). Hard Severe (3c, 4a, 4a).

Craig Y Castell from the road.

Creagh Dhu Wall – Description

It interests me to note that only the second route to be put up at Tremadog was pioneered by Johnny Cunningham and the Creagh Dhu. They referred to it in derogatory terms, which of course one would naturally expect, the climb being on the wrong side of the border.

As a Lakelander, viewing a Scot's climb in Wales, perhaps I can be a little fairer in my appraisal. The facts are that some 43 years later the climb remains, for its grade, one of the best little climbs in Wales. A pure rock climb, where each move is intrinsically good. It is steep and clean with the crystalline Tremadog rock giving great friction and good sharp jugs.

Stances with tree belays allow you enough space to throw off your pinching footwear and comfortably enjoy the crag's sunny disposition.

Immediately technical, a steep groove is followed until a swing out at the top leads across an exposed slab to a crack and good ledge. This is a pitch of contrast but the remainder of the climb gives constant exposure. From the tree ledge a hand traverse leads to a decidedly bold pull onto a pinnacle. Above it is steep and not a little intimidating. The crux, on the final pitch, involves a pull into a polished and insecure niche.

The rock dries instantly, gets much of the

sunshine this low-lying coastal crag has to offer, and can be climbed, enjoyably, twelve months of the year. Creagh Dhu Wall is a veritable route for all seasons.

Possibly it is because of the lack of such opportunity north of the Border that Cunningham chose to climb that frightening, vertical and brittle frozen water for which he is so famous. Surely that is the only reason imaginable for anyone wanting to climb ice?

Above left: **A balancy traverse on the first pitch of Creagh Dhu Wall.**
Above right: **John Adams starting the airy second pitch.**

WALES: Bomb Bay and Front Line

BOMB BAY: 60ft (18m). Very Severe (4c). **FRONT LINE:** 110ft (34m). Very Severe (4c).

BOMB BAY: 60ft (18m). Very Severe (4c).
First Ascent: P. Whillance, D. Armstrong, 2 January 1978.
FRONT LINE: 110ft (34m). Very Severe (4c)
First Ascent: P. Whillance, D. Armstrong, J. Lamb, 31 December 1976.
Location: South-west face, St. Govan's Head, Pembrokeshire.
Map Ref: 975927.
Guidebook: *Pembroke* by Jon de Montjoye and Mike Harber.
Attitude: Sea cliff, faces south.
Rock: Juggy limestone.
Access: South-west face of St. Govan's lies just outside the village of Bosherston (camping at vicarage or farm three miles (5km) before). It is the most accessible area and is four minutes' walk eastwards along top of cliff from St.

Govan's Chapel car park. Descend down a chimney (Difficult) formed by a stack, up which the climbs lie. The climbs are non-tidal, but lie within an army range. It is often open, however, when others may be closed. Holidays and weekends it is open; if in doubt 'phone Merrion Camp on Castlemartin 321.

Bomb Bay and Front Line – Summary

The climbs lie just left of the descent chimney. Bomb Bay is the first very obvious scoop—the right hand of two cracks. Front Line lies to the left on the edge of the wall up a beautiful-looking corner. Individual description is unnecessary, the climbs are one pitch straight up, although Front Line starts from

the left to gain the corner and climbs up high before stepping right where the corner disjoints.

Bomb Bay and Front Line – Description

Pembroke is a relatively new climbing ground and most of the routes are hard, but it's a very interesting area with a charm all of its own. The climbs, although short, are consistently brilliant and the limestone, sometimes requiring care, offers good positive holds. The two climbs chosen are very steep, deceptively so, but sport sound rock, big holds, and good protection.

Although there have been many contribu-

Above left: **Bill Birkett in the initial groove of Bomb Bay.**
Above right: **Wilf Williamson on the wall before the final groove of Front Line.**

tors, in terms of first ascensionists, to the area, the (then) Carlisle- (Lakeland-) based team of D. Armstrong, P. Botterill, J. Lamb and P. Whillance, driven south by the unsuitable winter weather for mountain rock climbing, probably did more than any other group to expose the vast potential of the south Pembroke coast. They were a 'hard' crew, but friendly and approachable, none more so than the 'gentle giant'—Jeff Lamb. Here was a man, a brilliant climber, to whom climbing was life, yet he was always ready to share his experiences, to talk, to be friendly, to laugh.

I last met Jeff Lamb high in the mountains, on the East Buttress of Scafell. Fit and lean, he ran round to the foot of where we were climbing simply to have a chat. Typically, his enthusiasm was sincere and his modesty, for a climber who had accomplished so much, refreshing. Shortly afterwards Jeff left for Australia where he died. His friends thought it to be the end of an era. These two routes, whatever their size or relative merits, are a part of that era.

I've included Bomb Bay to woo the newcomer. It has that approachable feeling with its niche-like belly pocketed with obvious holds. When you tackle it don't be put off by its strenuosity; it's not you, it really is steep. This is how all the climbs here shape up, from below they look easy, short and inconsequential. But they aren't.

On Front Line you climb every inch of its meagre 110ft (34in). It's steep from the start, but relatively straightforward until the corner bulges and it is necessary to move onto a short vertical wall that bars access to the delectable-looking right-angled corner groove above. Good nut protection makes the difference and one feels confident to attack it swiftly. Although arm-wrenching, there are very good, hidden holes in this pocket-ridden limestone and this makes it enjoyable. The top groove gives magnificent climbing. Looking down there's nothing below you, only the sun glinting on the rock, the sea spray and that good feeling of commitment.

Although on first acquaintance these two routes, and St. Govan's in general, may appear insignificant you will be very pleasantly surprised when you climb them. Both are a good introduction to the area and, being non-tidal, can be approached any time of the day. Indeed, because of the sheltered nature of this particular bay of rock one can climb here almost any time of the year and this is a major attraction.

During holiday periods, especially Christ-

Left: **The top groove of Front Line.**

mas and New Year, some attention should be paid to the possibility of stonefall. There still remains some loose rock and the rocky, boulder-strewn, nature of the ground below makes it difficult to move rapidly out of range.

You won't be disappointed if you climb these two routes and you'll finish them with a sincere wish to climb more.

Above left: **Wilf Williamson in the recess on Bomb Bay.**
Above right: **The wall between Bomb Bay and Front Line with the sea beyond.**

WALES: Great Slab

GREAT SLAB: 600ft (183m). Very Severe (4c, 4a, 4b, −, −).

First Ascent: C. F. Kirkus, G. G. Macphee, 1930.

Location: West buttress of Clogwyn Du'r Arrdu, Snowdon, North Wales, Snowdonia National Park.

Map Ref: OS 600 550.

Guidebooks: *Clogwyn du'r Arrdu* by Alec Sharp. *Snowdonia Rock Climbs* by Paul Williams.

Attitude: Faces north, only gets early morning and late evening sun.

Altitude: 2,300 ft (701m).

Rock: Volcanic tuff, generally good flake holds requiring care in places.

Access: From Llanberis follow the narrow road opposite the Royal Victoria Hotel (just above the Snowdon railway station). Go over a cattle grid and up the steep hill, through a gate near the top. Continue to pass under the Snowdon railway, gate, and on through another gate to a very small parking area. (It may be necessary to park at the top of the initial hill and pick up the Snowdon footpath which starts from here.) Up the grass slope, over a stile, to the railway track. Follow until its junction with the main footpath. Continue along passing Halfway House (tea and snacks may be purchased) until the miners' track breaks right and leads to the foot of the cliffs. The west buttress lies over on the right-hand side (45 minutes).

On weekends and holidays *beware of stonefall*.

Descent: Down the large rake, Western Terrace, slanting up rightwards below the West Buttress.

Great Slab – Summary

About 150ft (46m) up the Western Terrace a short slab sneaks leftwards providing an obvious break in the overhangs. Start from and belay to, a small rock pillar.

1. 130ft (40m), (4c). Step up from the pillar to reach a thin crack. Place a runner high in this then step back to traverse delicately left across the sandwiched slab (crux) to gain the long bottomless groove. Up the groove and continuation slab to a big ledge and thread belay between the blocks.

2. 130ft (40m), (4a). Go right to the rib and up this for 40ft. Go right to beneath a small overlap and continue up and right over mixed ground to belay below the Forty Foot Corner.

3. 60ft (18m), (4b). Up the corner, with a move left at half height, and at the top go left to belay (crux pitch if wet).

4, 5. 280ft (85m). Continue diagonally up and across the huge slab, eventually gaining the exposed left edge which is followed to the top.

Great Slab – Description

Clogwyn du'r Arddu, the Black Cliff, is unarguably one of Britain's greatest mountain crags and one of the most demanding. It is primarily a hard rock climber's crag, the climbs beginning at Very Severe and ending high in the extreme category.

George Abraham wrote (British Mountain Climbs, 1909);

'It cannot be said that this imposing mass possesses much prolonged interest for the rock-climber. It has been truly said that the easy places are too easy and the difficult places are impossible. However, a splendid day can be spent here exploring the face and revelling in probably the finest rock-scenery that Snowdon affords.'

The crag, in fact, features a number of distinctive styles of rock architecture and, today, Abraham's 'difficult places' host a variety of superb rock climbs. Blank walls, steep cracks, horizontal overhangs, blind grooves, deep chimneys and soaring aretes, curving buttresses, revealing ramps and huge slabs, some 500ft (152m) in length, are all to be found here.

There have been a number of significant stages in the crag's development, not the least when Joe Brown and Don Whillans climbed with earnest on these 'difficult places', and in doing so, established their reputation as leading British rock climbers of the 1950s and early 60s. They made Cloggy the mecca for 'hard men' and their excellent routes have popularised the crag to its present extent. But for many it is still the large leaning slabs of the West Buttress which most represent 'Cloggy' climbing.

Great Slab climbs the heart of the West Buttress and is, I found, a very pleasant introduction to the vastness of the place. To get to it one passes along under the rest of the cliff. This gives the ideal opportunity to stop and work out where the proliferation of famous lines lie; Woubits on the Far East Buttress, Shrike on the Gully Wall, Pinnacle Arete on the Pinnacle, Lithrig, Great Wall, Masters Wall, Vember, Curving crack, Troach, Cloggy Corner on the East Buttress, The Boldest on the Boulder, White Slab on the West Buttress. These and a host of others, are all great climbs irrespective of their varying degrees of difficulty. However, standing beneath Cloggy, especially during busy periods, can be dangerous and extreme care should be taken to watch out for stonefall. (A safety helmet is more valid here than on any other cliff in Britain that I have encountered.)

When reached, the whole of the West Buttress is found to be undercut and starting

GREAT SLAB

severe slabs (280ft)

Wet Corner

crux

belay point

T PAVEY 1985

GREAT SLAB: 600ft (183m).
Very Severe (4c, 4a, 4b, -, -,).

Clogwyn Du'r Arddu (the black cliff).

the routes problematical. This is the case on Great Slab where the crux is encountered in the first few feet. Afterwards the climb is technically less demanding, unless the 40-ft (12m) corner is wet, and very enjoyable, at about Severe in standard, although the climb remains a serious proposition throughout.

Serious because it is a big cliff, with some friable rock where a lot can happen, not least to the mountain weather, during the time spent on the face. And because of the leftward slant of the slabs between vertical walls, combined with the fact that the ground below drops away alarmingly quickly, a retreat from the West Buttress is not straightforward. A vertical abseil may take you over an edge, leaving you suspended in space, above the next slab system or above overhangs which separate the start of the slabs from the ground. There is an acute danger, because of the increased space, that your ropes may not be long enough to reach either the ground or the next suitable abseil point.

However, when you're young, ridiculously enthusiastic and in love with climbing, purely

for climbing's sake, seriousness is your very last consideration. This was the case when I tackled my first route on Cloggy—Great Slab. I remember finding the crux reasonable and afterwards racing up the upper slabs, drinking up the exposure for sure, but at the same time lusting for the next climb. The weather was good, the rock dry, vegetation uprooted and holds generally clean and sound.

I thoroughly enjoyed the climb, though it isn't fully adequate or fair to describe the climb in this simple way. Better to recall the adventures and emotions of Colin Kirkus as he broke his way for the first time (accompanied by the most famous of all anchor men G. G. Macphee), through the overhanging barrier, and threaded his way into the unknown regions of the massive slabs of the West Buttress. Kirkus wrote in his book *Let's Go Climbing* (Nelson, 1941).

'On Snowdon there is a cliff called Clogwyn d'ur Arddu. Its name is enough to frighten away many people. It is over 500 feet in height and mostly vertical—quite the most magnificent precipice in England and Wales.

Above left: **Don Whillans and Bill Peascod on the crux**.
Above right: **Don Whillans in the groove, first pitch**.

On the upper half of the buttress was a huge slab. If only it could be reached! Below, the rocks were almost vertical. But the main problem was in the first few feet.

The traverse was Very Severe. There was one sloping hold where my rubbers would not grip at all, so at last I took them off and managed to get across in my stockinged feet.

I found myself on a tiny grass ledge, looking rather hopelessly up at the grim face above. I had crossed on to a higher part of the cliff and was already 100 feet above the bottom, with the overhang below me. I felt very small and isolated.

I started up the narrow slab. It was far more difficult than it had looked and wickedly rotten. I threw down every other hold. A thin ribbon of grass ran all the way up on the right, looking like a long and rugged caterpillar. I thought that even this might

be safer than the rock and plunged into it. It wasn't at all a friendly kind of caterpillar; it began to peel off and slide down. I left this moving staircase very hurriedly, and took to the rocks again. I climbed on the extreme edge, where it seemed to be a little firmer. Below my left foot the rocks dropped, sheer and unclimbable, for 200 feet.

Macphee called up that I had run out nearly all of the 120 foot line. There was no stance in sight, so I had to stand about uncomfortably while he tied on another 100-foot length. I went on and on, with things looking more and more hopeless. I wondered whether I should ever find a belay.

At last the climbing began to get easier, and I was able to traverse to a sheltered grassy recess on the left. There was a perfect thread-belay, and Macphee soon joined me. It was wonderful to think that no one had ever been here before. It was still more

63

interesting to wonder whether we should ever escape.'

Thus Colin Kirkus described the first pitch of Great Slab. An incredible adventure and a significant breakthrough in Welsh climbing history. He concluded his story:

'But it had been a marvellous day. We had done 1000 feet of rock-climbing* most of it in the Very Severe class.

No one else can have the thrill of the first ascent.'

The seriousness of Cloggy, experienced by Kirkus, had always eluded me until I returned, on 17 May 1985, to Great Slab. My intent was to photograph the route with two of the all time greats of British rock climbing; my good friends Bill Peascod and Don Whillans. Sometimes you hit it off with people and sometimes you don't. Bill, Don and myself, although many years apart in age, did.

Bill genuinely bubbled with enthusiasm and Don, the legendary figure of both rock climbing and mountaineering, seemed infected with the spirit of it. I felt, somehow, there was something very special here—it was as though a giant, tired by experience, had again awakened with fresh eyes. Bill had written in his autobiography *(Journey After Dawn)*:

*They had climbed 'Longland's Climb' earlier in the day.

"Next year," said Don, "as soon as the nice weather gets here, and when it's still quiet, come down for a couple of weeks and we'll have a good look round. We'll nip down to Pembroke and maybe Cornwall; it's grand there—and we'll go up to Cloggy and see what's going on . . ."

A while after this, when things were being fixed up, Don said to me, 'You come too. Aye as well as getting your photographs I've a new route to do in the quarry behind my house (at Penmaenmawr), you can lead us up 'em.'

As we drove up to Cloggy we laughed at the fact that the day was fine and it was going to be on and the fact that we were all Taureans with our birthdays separated by barely a week. At the crag the bottom pitch was inevitably weeping water beneath the overhang. Consequently the crux approach slab beneath was wet.

Don started off from the flake pinnacle where Bill was delayed. Stepping up, then across, he met with the insipid dampness and came back down. Bill asked with a wink if he should take over the lead. Only Bill was in a position (psychologically) to do this. In reply, Don flitted up and across as nimbly as I've seen anyone climb and up to the belay 120ft (31m) above.

As middleman, Bill set off, pausing only to say directly to me, 'I'm going to fall off this mate.' Yet he went up and across, dancing those delicate moves in the beautiful Peascod fashion. Stopping after the crux to smile he then moved across to the easy groove. Here he slumped on to the rope and died. Three months later Don died, too.

Cloggy does seem serious to me now. But there are still a good few lines for me to do and I intend to return. I suppose when you're older, ridiculously enthusiastic and in love with climbing, purely for climbing's sake, seriousness is the very last consideration.

WALES: Direct Route

DIRECT ROUTE: 245ft (75m). Very Severe. (4a, 4b, 4c, 5b or aid).
First Ascent: C.F. Kirkus, J.B. Dodd, 1930.
Location: Dinas Mot, south side of Llanberis Pass, North Wales, Snowdonia National Park (Opposite Dinas Cromlech).
Map Ref: 0S 626563.
Guidebooks: *Llanberis Pass* by Geoff Milburn. *Snowdonia Rock Climbs* by Paul Williams.
Attitude: Faces north.
Altitude: 700ft (213m).
Rock: Rhyolite.
Access: From the lay-by (Pont Y Cromlech car park) go over the wall, across the river and follow the obvious path via any number of wooden stiles (12 minutes).
Descent: From the top of the climb traverse right to gain the large cleft. Descend down this—easy climbing. (Western Gully—graded Moderate.)

Direct Route – Summary

Takes the most obvious shallow groove in the centre of the Nose. From the lowest point of the buttress scramble up to the right to belay on a flat-topped pedestal.

1. 140ft (43m), (4b). Step up into a groove and after a few feet move round the rib to gain a ledge (possible poor belay). Go up rightwards to the light-coloured groove. Follow the ramp leftwards then step back into the groove. Up with difficulty over a bulge to gain a large scooped stance.

2. 50ft (15m), (4c). Up easily then go right on good holds to the obvious steep diagonal finger crack traverse leading rightwards. Follow this, then straight up to a long thin ledge and great belays.

3. 55ft (17m), (5b). The corner on the left is

Llanberis Pass.

65

DIRECT ROUTE

possible
belay

○ belay point

**DIRECT ROUTE: 245ft (75m). Very
Severe. (4a, 4b, 4c, 5b or aid).**

hard to start. Wide precarious bridging (crux)
to a good hold or combined tactics or a lassoo.
Continue up the jammed flake splinter to finish
up a short corner.

Direct Route – Description

The clean lightish area of rock which forms
the central lower area of the extensive Dinas
Mot does not run to striking-looking lines. In
this and other ways it could be considered as a
direct contrast to its opposite neighbour,
Dinas Cromlech, on the other side of the Pass.
The Cromlech is spectacular, the Mot rather
ordinary-looking, the former obvious, the
latter quite subtle.

From the road, only a few minutes' easy
walk away, one line does suggest itself as being
more obvious than the rest. It's situated,
correctly so, dead centre and runs without
deviation directly from bottom to top. It is
Colin Kirkus's Direct Route and ranks
alongside the best rock climbs in Wales.

Quality of climbing is exceptional and
throughout its 200-ft-plus (61-m) length the
variety of techniques employed make it a
technically demanding lead for its grade.
Almost very type of climbing move can be
employed on this route in a delightful sequence, the balance and mix of which seem just
right for maximum satisfaction.

If there is a predominant single technique it
is that of bold balance climbing, but even this
is interspaced with finger pulling on pockets
and incut holds. To these moves can be added
finger and hand jamming, and for the feet,
bridging and smearing. Feet and hands are
used in unison when laybacking and moves at
the top can be chimneyed.

The first main section of climbing is proof of
the fact that Kirkus was a bold climber. Even
with modern nuts, protection is spaced, and a
steady approach is essential. Holds are always
small—I remember pulling up on a two-finger
pocket at one stage—but they are adequate.

Despite its great popularity the rock, although well worn, remains rough and the friction is good.

Another characteristic of this early section is the tight, homogenuous, nature of the rock. Holds are recessed; pockets, slits or occasionally hand ledges, rather than sharp flakes or jug handles. Despite this there are just enough features—a shallow groove, a ramp, a niche—to make the line fit together and low at the Very Severe grade.

The next pitch, issuing from the heart of the buttress, is much photographed and written about, but one still needs to climb it to know it. The finger traverse is both strenuous and delicate; requiring a degree of commitment. Soon a commodious ledge is reached where one can sit, in civilised fashion, and discuss the prospects of the next and crux pitch.

We were joined here by a bedraggled-looking figure who had battled his way, in cold, damp conditions, up the Super Direct. There was plenty of room and we didn't begrudge his presence. He eyed our final pitch wistfully.

No wonder, its attractions are obvious even from the side. A huge splintered flake, 35ft (11m) high and 3ft (1m) broad, stands in the corner, only its base doesn't reach the ledge and the corner is tight below. These few feet, climbed free (5b) constitute the very hard crux. Traditionally the move was effected using combined tactics—with Kirkus standing on the shoulders of J.B. Dodd. They reported: 'Time taken 4 to 5 hours—should long remain a record. A ladder would make the final crack suitable for others than a few rock gymnasts.'

If you don't climb 5b or you don't have a very long reach, then aid in the form of a shoulder, or lassoing the spike, is still commonly employed. Climbing the moves free involve wide bridging, or as Cris Ann said, much to our amusement, 'Hey man, crazy stemming.' Above, the flake can again be tackled 'Yosemite' style by 'laying away' and hand jamming or even the quaint old English techniques of 'monkey on a stick' ending with 'backing and footing'.

Funny nobody accredited Kirkus with all these techniques. But then, I suppose, it was sufficient for him to mention, in those days, just that it was a rather fine climb.

WALES: Mur Y Niwl and Pinnacle Wall (Combination)

MUR Y NIWL: 250ft (76m). Very Severe (4b, 4c, –).
First Ascent: A.J.J. Moulam and J.B. Churchill, 1952.

Darrel Crilley: The hand traverse, second pitch, Mur Y Niwl.

PINNACLE WALL: 230ft (70m). Severe.
First Ascent: C.F. Kirkus (Solo), 1931.
Location: Amphitheatre and Pinnacle Walls of Craig Yr Ysfa, situated high on the side of Carnedd Llewelyn, above the Ogwen Valley, North Wales, Snowdonia National Park (near Capel Curig).
Map Ref: 694637.
Guidebooks: *Carneddau* by Les Holliwell (Climbers' Club). *Snowdonia Rock Climbs* by Paul Williams.
Attitude: Faces south east. Altitude: 2300ft (701m).
Rock: Rhyolite, giving sharp holds.
Access: Follow a surfaced road from a gate on the north side of the A5 (0S 687603). Where it goes left continue straight on, on a path which rises to skirt the right side of the Ffynnon Llugwy reservoir. Going steeply up to a Col (695633), the cliff can now be seen on the right side of Carnedd Llewelyn. To gain the climbs on the Amphitheatre Wall (the large wall right of the obvious amphitheatre), continue along the Col and up to above the amphitheatre itself. Descend steeply down keeping to the 'Wall' side (left side looking out) of the amphitheatre. Steep scree and grass give way to rocks of moderate difficulty. Not particularly difficult but care should be exercised.

Mur Y Niwl – Summary

This climb leads to the bottom of the Pinnacle Wall. Start in the gully right of a small chimney and left of a long grass ledge situated 15ft (6m) above the bed of the gully.

1. 40ft (12m), (4b). Up to gain the ledge. Belay on the right end.

2. 100ft (30m), (4c). Climb the wall to a niche, step right and up (better holds) to base of a V-groove. Follow the very obvious hand traverse rightwards and either follow this in its entirety to the 'perch' (hard) or move down and delicately right to a diagonal crack leading up to the 'perch' stance (old and dubious pegs).

3. 60ft (18m), (4c). Move down and right (sharp holds), below the overhang, to a ledge. Up and left to another ledge (peg runner). Follow the arete on the left to a stance and block belay.

4. 40ft (12m), (4b). Climb groove to glacis, go left to short cracked wall.

5. 90ft (27m), (4c). Up wall (awkward) to belay after a further 80ft (24m) at the base of the upper (Pinnacle) wall.

Pinnacle Wall – Summary

The logical continuation to Mur Y Niwl.

Start below a quartz ledge at a rightward leading (apparently grassy) corner.

1. 40ft (12m). Up stepped corner to a stance.

2. 90ft (27m). Go up for 10ft (3m) to a leftward quartz traverse until a balancy move, at the end, leads to a small stance.

3. 100ft (30m). Go up the corner for 30ft (9m) to a good and rough edged crack leading to the Pinnacle. Move left and up slab to finish.

Mur Y Niwl and Pinnacle Wall – Description

The climbing potential of Craig yr Ysfa, legend has it, was first discovered when the crag was viewed, by chance, through a telescope from the summit of Scafell. A rather ignominious beginning for a Welsh cliff! That apart, the fact that the cliff held the eye at such a distance is an indication of its size. It is huge, remote, complex, but unfortunately rather broken.

Climbing development followed the classical pattern of first gullies and then the buttresses but unlike its once famous counterparts, Lliwedd and Clogwyn Y Ddysgl on the Snowdon massif, the crag has remained relatively popular. Justifiably so, for the Amphitheatre Wall and Pinnacle Wall, perched immediately above, are spectacular vertical faces of rock; summated, giving a vertical fall of some 350ft (107m).

Mur Y Niwl (The Wall of Mists) and Pinnacle Wall form a natural and challenging climb, from bottom to top, of this incredibly exposed sheer cleft of rock. The former is at the very top end of its grade (indeed, it was originally given Hard Very Severe) and the latter a delightful climb—marked with a number of distinctive physical features. Both are incredibly exposed, with situations that demand full concentration.

The atmosphere is intense, the size of the wall seems unbelievable, heightened by a descent which demands respect. It's not so much difficult as, well, atmospheric. A dead sheep and distinctly streaky wet-looking rock marked the commencement of our ascent. We were both 'well psyched'.

Even the first few feet, up to the long grass ledge, have to be climbed. The rock is good, rough, and truly tough. Holds that should be good and incut tend to be flat and the angle soon informs the arms that work has to be done. As you venture further the immense exposure pulls at your ankles, but the climbing does not relent in difficulty. On the contrary, the hardest moves are yet to come.

A steep wall leads to an extreme-looking groove from where a great hand break escapes across the wall to the right. Over in the distance, above a wall that has no end, a head of rock, 'the perch', offers something tangible to go for. The traverse is strenuous, the moves wild, and the footholds are spaced and barely adequate. Somewhere near the end you're supposed to drop down to gain the corner crack emanating from the top of the 'perch'. We kept traversing, handholds were insecure and footwork demanding.

Two old pegs were clipped, nuts and friends

The third pitch, Mur Y Niwl.

MUR Y NIWL AND PINNACLE WALL

The Pinnacle

Pinnacle Wall

Mur Y Niwl

crux traverse

bottom obscured

○ belay point

Above: **MUR Y NIWL: 250ft (76m).**
Very Severe (4b, 4c, -). PINNACLE
WALL: 230ft (70m). Severe.
Right: **Stepping off the Pinnacle.**

placed, but the 'Perch' never felt homesome. Another strenuous 10ft (3m) and things became more like 'VS', but the interest was retained. First with a groove, where a one-finger pocket was the best hold to be had in the wet and then with a 10-ft (3-m) boulder problem wall leading to the Bilberry terrace.

Mur Y Niwl, the wall of mists—a beautiful name. I would have excused the first ascensionists if they had named it 'the great big wall of unbelievable exposure and hard climbing'. You think that's ridiculous?—go and try it!

Logically the follow on up the wall above is by the Pinnacle Wall, a full and interesting climb in its own right. The rock sharp with crystals and rough knobbles, is a delight to climb on and the position is incredibly airy.

An easy corner ramp of no particular interest provides the opening key to the wall and leads to a great white quartz shelf, about 3ft (1m) wide. This stretches, like some magical carpet in space, falls gently away from you for some 90ft (27m). At the end a corner rises munificently above.

The corner is followed, steeply, until a crack, invisible from below, gives access to the pinnacle. Tapering from its grandiose base, the pinnacle stands detached, some 30ft (9m) high. The final move made from its tip is as from the point of a needle—a perfect pinnacle and a superb route. Possibly the most delectable and balanced solo first ascent in Britain.

Trust the 'Lakes' lads' to know a good crag when they see one.

70

WALES: Blanco

BLANCO: 240ft (73m). Hard Very Severe (4c, 5a, 4a).
First Ascent: Joe Brown, Dave Alcock, 15 September 1966.
Location: Castell Helen, South Stack, Gogarth, Anglesey, Wales.
Map Ref: 207818.
Guidebook: *Gogarth* by Alec Sharp (Climbers' Club).
Attitude: Sea cliff, faces south west. No seasonal restrictions.
Rock: Quartzite.
Access: Approach from the top South Stack car park down a distinct track to the recently refurbished Helen's Cottage (now used for bird watching). To the right (looking out) and down another 40ft (12m) there is a small ledge and in situ pegs (use nut back up) giving the first abseil (120ft, 37m). Aim for a distinct ledge on the right (looking in). From here (90ft, 27m) abseil leftwards to gain the only rock shelf below the cliff. If covered by sea, abseil leftwards (or climb across at sea level) to a large niche (5 minutes).

Blanco – Summary

The line gains and follows an obvious corner/groove leading diagonally leftwards to the overlaps near the arete. It breaks through these to follow a distinct crack leading to the arete.

1. 60ft (18m), (4c). Climb straight up the niche and continue until you move left, then up again and gain the largest quartz band. Belay on this (just about the top of the niche). The shallow groove straight above is Poseidon (VS).

2. 100ft (30m), (5a). Follow the corner/groove diagonally leftwards and break through first overlap to start of crack. Up and through second (main) overlap to gain the distinct steep crack. Climb this to arete, ledge and belay.

3. 80ft (24m), (4a). Up the arete and then rightwards to finish at the first abseil point.

Blanco – Description

I must admit that Anglesey/Gogarth is one of my favourite cliffs. When I was a lad it was the 'in place', where everything was happening. Today the total adventure of the sea, the lines, the rock and the environment all still hold a fascination for me.

Castell Helen gives the best rock in the South Stack area (North Stack is even better) being of hard quartzite seamed with quartz bands. It's a place you can climb most days and gets sunshine from early morning even in winter. When the wind screams at Helen's Cottage you can still be climbing in tee-shirt and shorts down below—honest.

BLANCO: 240ft (73m). Hard Very Severe (4c, 5a, 4a).

BLANCO

line other side of arete

crux

2nd pitch

niche

1st pitch

belay point

Gogarth climbing is always steep but the secret is that the holds are generally magnificent; great hidden pockets, chunky flakes, biscuits to pinch and spikes to skewer yourself on. (But be cautious, the rock doesn't have the strength of the volcanics.) The route Blanco, whilst one of the easier climbs, captures much that is good and unique to these cliffs. It's a Joe Brown and Dave Alcock line which guarantees it is great. Looking up the wall from sea level gives one the impression that the climbing is going to be formidable. Firstly it is a very large wall, secondly those overhangs look desperate and thirdly the sea, lapping threatening at your feet, heightens the sense of panic. However, the climbing is much easier than appearances suggest. That's not to say it's without interest, for there are some technical moves to be accomplished, just that it is possible within the Hard Very Severe grade.

The first pitch involves a traverse left, from the top of the niche, to gain the quartz band and hanging belay and this does make you think it's steep ground, but the holds are satisfactory. Yet only on the hottest and sunniest of days does that sea soapy feel ever completely disappear and this is another factor to be reckoned with when climbing on the Gogarth Sea Cliffs.

It is the second pitch that is the big one. After a steep groove, where the exposure and your vulnerability begin to tell, you arrive below the overhangs. Here the position is uncompromising, but the holds, and they are good, are always just as far away as your next reach. (Friend protection recommended below the biggest overlap.) The solution to the overhangs is surprisingly simple and it is this transition of fear being replaced with pleasure that gives the route much of its character. Above the overhangs a wide crack carries you quickly, if somewhat boldly, to a superb position on the hanging arete.

The next section is very reasonable climbing, but one should maintain concentration—for a dash of loose rock and a scattering of seaside greenery could easily unbalance the complacent. When you pull over the top you're back in the crowded world, but other than this the situation couldn't be finer. A host of gulls, fulmars and guillemots swoop and dive, white horses play below and a fresh sea breeze licks your face. The change from vertical to horizontal is complete.

Left: **Tony Brindle and Denise Stratton tackling the first pitch from the sea.**

There was a time when Joe Brown was thought to be at the climbing limit. All that's changed rapidly but what remains is much better; the fact that he climbed stupendous natural lines, and the enjoyment of these routes. Blanco in its own small way is the truth behind the legend.

Above left: **Denise Stratton completing the first pitch, South Stack Lighthouse in the background.**
Above right: **Abseiling from half-way ledge.**

WALES: Cenotaph Corner, Left Wall, Right Wall

Above left: **Paul Cornforth committing himself on Right Wall.**

Above right: **Approaching a large pocket and the first crux on Right Wall.**

CENOTAPH CORNER: 120ft (37m), (5b), E1.
First Ascent: Joe Brown, Doug Belshaw, 1952.
LEFT WALL: 130ft (40m), (5c), E2.
First Ascent: R. Moseley, J. Smith, J. Sutherland, 1956.
RIGHT WALL: 150ft (46m), (6a), E5.
First Ascent: Pete Livesey, 1974.
Location: Dinas Cromlech, north side of Llanberis Pass, North Wales, Snowdonia National Park.
Map Ref: 629569.
Guidebooks: *Llanberis* by Geoff Milburn (Climbers' Club),
Snowdonia Rock Climbs by Paul Williams.

Attitude: Faces south west.
Altitude: 1000ft (305m).
Rock: Rough mountain Rhyolite.
Access: The Llanberis Pass, the most popular climbing area in Snowdonia, forms the rocky valley between Snowdon and the Glyders. Along the A4086 from Llanberis to Pen Y Pass Dinas Cromlech is the last imposing cliff on the left-hand side (north). It stands unmistakenly above Pont Y Cromlech bridge and is reached from the lay-by directly below (20 minutes).
Descent: This is best effected by abseiling from the large tree-strewn ledge above the Right Wall (The Valley). Care must be taken with respect to parties below.

and nut belays directly above the crack. To finish scramble rightwards. Best to stay roped, and abseil from the valley or continue upwards to find a path which leads off way over to the left (looking in).

Left: **Low on the Left Wall.**

Right Wall – Summary

Scramble up to large rocky ledge as for the corner, then go up to a grassy ledge on the right. Above a short wall gives access to a shallow corner which issues a leftward-slanting crack.

1. 150ft (46m), (6a). Climb the short wall to ledge. Up shallow corner (from here it is possible to tie off the old bolt-heads) and go leftwards up the crack to a spike and nut runner. Step down right and then straight up on small pockets to a rightward rising finger ledge. Follow this to a resting ledge (nut on the right). Move up on square foothold then up and left to a large pocket (nut low down beneath pocket and Friend $2^1/_2$ over to left). Move up and left on small pockets (first crux) to the Girdle ledge. Traverse right to beneath the porthole, 20ft (6m) above the ledge. Up to this and step in it (second crux) to reach better holds which lead right. Keep going right to a thin crack which leads to the top.

Cenotaph Corner, Left Wall, Right Wall – Description

After considerable heartache I realised that not one of these three brilliant extreme climbs could be omitted. Each is intrinsically different and each one represents a landmark in the development of Welsh rock climbing. On top of this, of course, one reaches the crag and the climbing in a matter of minutes—ideal, then, for the rock star who doesn't care for diversions in the form of 'hill bashing'.

Cenotaph Corner, the obvious middle of my trio, has been described as the most famous climb in Britain. A perfect right-angled corner, it contains 120ft (37m) of distinctive and extremely well protected climbing. After 25ft (8m) one experiences the first difficult move and it is here that the unrelenting verticality of the crack above begins to prick the now enlivened senses. Hand jamming, bridging and laybacking are used in varying degrees depending on your personal preference, but all goes straightforwardly until a shallow niche is reached, tantalisingly near the top. On Joe Brown's first ascent, and for quite a few ascents afterwards, two pitons were employed here for aid. Now, of course, with no vegetation, with modern gear and enlightenment, it goes completely free and the moves couldn't be safer, but they are, most definitely, extreme.

Cenotaph Corner – Summary

The right-angled joining of the two sheer walls. Start after scrambling to the foot of the corner.

1. 120ft (37m), (5b). Straight up the corner. Difficult at 25ft (8m) and entering the niche at 90ft (27m). The crux is leaving the niche to regain the crack above.

Left Wall – Summary

Scramble to start on a large sloping rock ledge below and left of the corner.

1. 130ft (40m), (5c). Diagonally left to a shattered ledge below the crack. Follow this to a resting place below the fork. Up and take the left-hand branch which gives fingery climbing, with good protection, until easy moves left (not apparent from below) lead to left arete. Follow up and scramble back right, to thread

CENOTAPH CORNER,
LEFT WALL, RIGHT WALL

**CENOTAPH CORNER: 120ft
(37m), (5b), E1. LEFT WALL: 130ft
(40m), (5c), E2.
RIGHT WALL: 150ft (46m), (6a),
E5.**

On my ascent of the Corner, in the late 1960s, I bypassed the in situ bottom peg to find the peg above the niche had gone. Using the pocket, widened by its placement, I managed the moves free. Only sweating and jugs remain; the famous jug handle final hold, once referred to as being as big as Grecian urn, was reached ecstatically. Well I couldn't wait to get back to the Lakes and tell someone; Cenotaph Corner, free, was my huge ambition.

I told Peter Greenall, Rock and Ice man, in the Climbers' Shop. He retorted flatly, 'So what—it's already been done free by so and so a year ago.' I thought it didn't really bother me who had done it free and who hadn't—I knew I had. I bought a magazine and went off to sulk! OK, I guess it did bother me actually.

Left Wall was originally climbed with a fair amount of aid and was first free-climbed by Steven Wunsch (an American visitor) in 1972. It is now a contender to be one of the best single pitches in Britain. The impression,

looking up from the road, is that both the left and right walls of Cenotaph Corner are featureless and blank. As one draws nearer the Cromlech (the city of stone), a striking forked crack-line can be seen snaking up the Left Wall—its only natural line of weakness.

An impressive line in an impressive position, the steep ground rapidly tumbles away hundreds of feet to the Llanberis Pass below. The situation gives you a feeling of being 'out there' even before you launch onto what is obviously going to be a very big lead. However, if Cenotaph Corner is well protected by nuts, then Left Wall is doubly so. You can place as much protection as you're prepared to carry.

It's best not to dawdle as the verticality constantly strains the arms but, after 80ft (25m) or so, a good rest can be had below where the crack forks left (the right continuation is taken by Resurrection (E4) and is considerably harder). Continuing up the left-hand branch constitutes the crux, but the small

Above left: **Chris Ann Crysdale tackling the difficult moves at 30ft on Cenotaph Corner.** Above right: **Streaming wet conditions on Cenotaph Corner.**

footholds on the left, small fingerholds and sinking wire runners (stopper 4/Rock 2) soon lead to moves on big holds, to the left Arete and then it's all over. It's the sort of route you want to do again; safe, steep and honest with the wall and the crack providing solid incut flakes and sinking hand jams.

Right Wall is considerably neckier but it's an absolute landmark in British free rock climbing; more importantly, it's also an enjoyable climb of considerable quality. Pete Livesey was way ahead of the pack, in terms of producing difficult new routes, in 1974: Right Wall in Wales and Footless Crow in the Lakes heralded a new generation of high standard climbs and enlightened rock climbers. I say enlightened because Livesey showed what was possible with a little training and dedication and the application of modern rope and protection techniques. It wasn't that the popularly imagined 'Hard Man' approach of Brown and Whillans became less attractive, just that with the new dawn in standards, it could be put comfortably on the shelf, to be taken at leisure, rather than being regarded as

the established code for climbing success.

The Wall looks blank; it isn't quite. Good ledges, finger pockets and sharp flakes abound. The regular E5 climber will almost be embarrassed by their size and frequency, but when one's said all that, the route has still got to be climbed.

With Lark's tongue tie-offs and a wire looped around the heads of the 'pathetic' old expansion bolts the difficulties start and the moves up and right to the first resting ledge seem particularly serious. Left to the large pocket reveals a good nut and a Friend 2½ further over, but I couldn't be bothered fiddling about and quickly launched up on initially small, but rapidly increasing, pockets to reach the girdle ledge. Above, gaining and leaving the large 'porthole' is probably the crux of the climb, but the rest is a doddle and you will be soon belayed to the trees in the 'valley'.

Then you shout down to the diminutive figure below; 'Yeah it's easy—about Lakes E3 5c', relieved to be safe once again.

Above left: **Chris Ann Crysdale tackling the difficult moves at 30ft on Cenotaph Corner.** Above right: **Streaming wet conditions on Cenotaph Corner.**

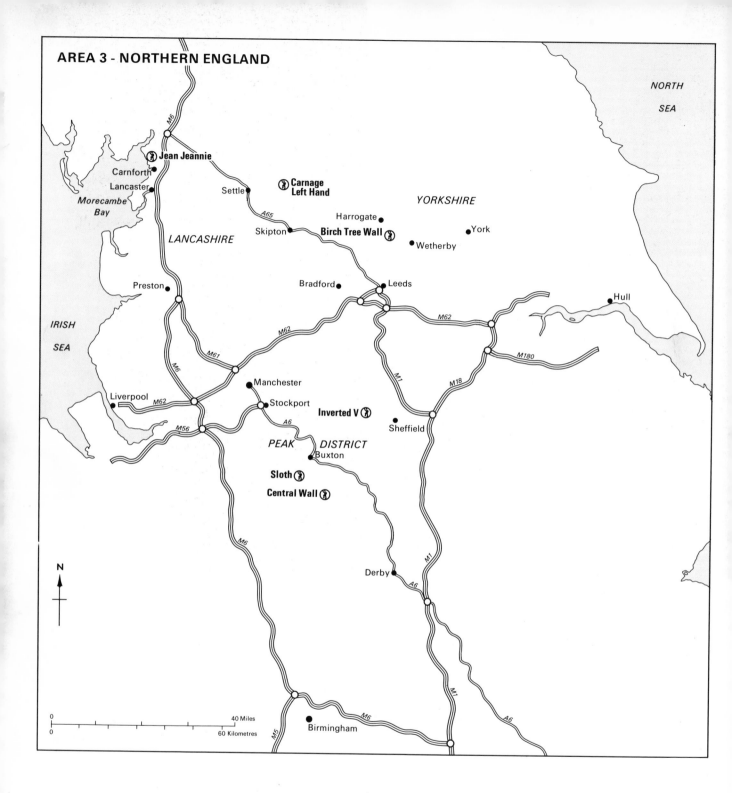

AREA 3 - NORTHERN ENGLAND

NORTH SEA

Jean Jeannie

Carnforth

Lancaster

Morecambe Bay

Settle

Carnage Left Hand

YORKSHIRE

Harrogate

LANCASHIRE

Skipton

Birch Tree Wall

Wetherby

York

IRISH SEA

Preston

Bradford

Leeds

Hull

M62

M61

M6

M62

M180

Liverpool

Manchester

M1

M18

M56

Stockport

Inverted V

A6

Sheffield

PEAK   DISTRICT

Buxton

Sloth

Central Wall

M6

N

Derby

M1

A6

0   40 Miles
0   60 Kilometres

M5

Birmingham

M6

M1

A6

NORTHERN ENGLAND: Black And Tans and The Sloth

BLACK AND TANS: 100ft (30m). Severe.
First Ascent: A.S. Piggot, *circa* 1923.
THE SLOTH: 90ft (27m). Hard Very Severe (5a).
First Ascent: Don Whillans, *circa* 1950s.
Location: Roaches Upper Tier, Staffordshire, Peak District National Park, 4.5 miles (7km) north of Leek and 10 miles (16km) south-west of Buxton.
Map Ref: 005623.
Guidebooks: *Staffordshire Area* by British Mountaineering Council, *Rock Climbing in The Peak District* by Paul Nunn.
Attitude: West facing, situated on the south-western edge of the high gritstone moorland.

Altitude: 150ft (46m).
Rock: Millstone grit.
Access: From the A53 turn off to drive through Upper Hulme. Shortly afterwards Hen Cloud and then the Roaches can be seen up above. A large lay-by lies directly below the Roaches. From this follow the path, past a walled garden and Duggie's cottage (Duggie is a character who may often be seen wandering around the rocks with a large axe and wild expression—but enjoys a 'crack' and will always direct you to any climb). Take the stone steps to the upper tier where the highest part of the buttress holds the climbs (10 minutes).

Above left: **Tim Valley making one of the three bold and precarious mantleshelf moves on Black and Tans.**
Above right: **John White hanging from the roof on The Sloth.**

BLACK AND TANS AND THE SLOTH

(labels on illustration)
3 mantle shelves
Black & Tans
Sloth
belay point
T PAVEY 1985

BLACK AND TANS: 100ft (30m). Severe. THE SLOTH: 90ft (27m). Hard Very Severe (5a).

Black and Tans – Summary

Start in a chimney containing a holly tree.

1. 50ft (15m). Move up a few feet then swing left onto a ledge below the corner. Up to a long narrow ledge, belay on left below big corner.

2. 50ft (15m). Up to the roof, move left onto the nose and go straight up this making three precarious and bold mantleshelf moves.

The Sloth – Summary

1. 90ft (27m), (5a). Move up the wall to gain the flake crack on the right of the Pedestal flake. From the top of the Pedestal climb a narrow crack to the roof. The huge flake block on the left takes a long sling runner before exciting moves along the roof lead to a wide crack, a flared chimney, ledges and thread belays.

Black And Tans and The Sloth – Description

There are a few routes which epitomise the nature of a crag or a type of rock or a style of climbing or, even, reflect the character of the first ascensionists. These are the great routes, they linger in the memory of old men and become the ambition of the young. Sloth has all the above qualities and, rightly is one of the most famous routes on gritstone.

The Roaches is a rugged natural outcrop of impeccable rock, offering a wide variety of holds and types of climbing—one of the best and most popular of the grit outcrops. At its highest point the vertical wall veers outwards into space and forms a heart-stopping roof. One crack breaks through the barrier and this is the line of 'The Sloth'.

First climb up the wall by utilising the attractive jamming cracks to gain a distinct small ledge—the pedestal. Now when the exposure makes itself felt the climbing becomes hard.

The roof looks frighteningly desperate, black, menacing, precarious and strenuous. Gain the roof, steeply, up a thinning vertical crack, then, on the left, where steep becomes overhanging, a great sling can be placed behind a solid boss of grit. A reach right enables the obvious large thin flake to be gripped; it's good but sounds alarmingly hollow. Gravity now pulls at your feet and positive action is required to stop them swinging into the void below. So sort them out, find some holds and it's then that your body assumes the horizontal. You go along that great ceiling of rock until your head emerges round the lip and with pumping arms and racing heart you jam an ever-widening vertical crack to caves, ledges and respite.

The line is direct, obvious and challenging; no climber can pass it by without feeling its pull. Once tackled and commitment made, its execution proves to be a super sequence of exciting moves on very reasonable holds; but making that commitment is a very intimidating experience.

Some of the character of Don Whillans is certainly reflected in Sloth. The hard and bold nature for sure, but also for those that climb the route and knew the man a little better it transmits qualities of ingenuity and understanding.

'It's easy if you use your loaf.'

Black and Tans is a vastly different proposition, but is still a fine climb in its own right. One of the longest routes (exclusive of girdles) on gritstone it packs in a good variety of sound climbing. A tricky move onto a ledge starts the climbing and leads to a layback groove. After the easy traverse it is usual to belay below the attractive corner. Moves left from the top of this lead to the exposed nose and the three infamous mantleshelf moves of sparse protection and increasing difficulty. An excellent little route.

Tim Valley in the first groove of Black and Tans.

INVERTED V: 70ft (21m). Very Severe (4b).
RIGHT-HAND BUTTRESS: 75ft (23m). Severe (3c).

First Ascent: Cyril Ward in early 1920s.
Location: Southern end Stanage Edge, Peak District.
Map Ref: 247832.
Guidebooks: *Rock Climbing in the Peak District* by Paul Nunn, *Stanage/Millstone*— BMC (1983).
Rock: Gritstone.
Access: The classic grit edge, Stanage, extends for 4 miles (6km). The above climbs lie at its most accessible, southerly, end. Fifteen minutes' walk from car.

Catherine Destivelle high on Inverted V.

Inverted V – Summary

The route is easily identifiable. Jam up the corner to a bulge, continue to below the roof. Traverse left and easily up.

Right-Hand Buttress – Summary

The big grit crack right of Inverted V. It virtually splits the buttress. Up under the roof until moves right enable a mantleshelf move to gain a ledge below the crack. The crack is smooth, continuous and awkward in places.

Inverted V and Right-Hand Buttress – Description

Considering the wealth and diversity of British rock, cliffs and climbing, it may appear something of a paradox that gritstone, so slight in form, plays such an important role in colouring the national character of our climbing. Certainly its accessibility to large centres of population, the steel city of Sheffield and the cotton town of Manchester, plays its part. Even so probably the most single influencing feature is the geological uniqueness of the rock and consequent nature of the climbing.

Gritstone is a mixture of sharp angular Silica cemented together, from sand size through to small pebbles. Rough and strong, its climbing features range from friction slabs, through pebble-holds-only walls, to jamming cracks (both vertical and horizontal). To perform well on grit one must develop a smooth flowing, confident, style and master a number of diverse techniques: that of balance climbing, of pressure-hold climbing (palming, laying away and mantling all on rounded edges) and the most famous of all, the technique of hand jamming.

Many of our 'greats' started and trained on gritstone; Piggot, Kelly, Dolphin, Brown and

Inverted V

Right-Hand Buttress

O belay point

Fawcett to name but a handful. From these early grit days their influence spread both nationally and internationally—the techniques mastered on grit proving fundamental to high performance elsewhere.

Of course Stanage is *the* gritstone edge. Stretching for 4 miles (6km) it is quick drying and offers the complete range of gritstone climbing at all standards. The rock structure is varied and there are some 648 routes recorded in the 1983 guidebook. To choose two routes on one crag of over 600, to choose one crag from the many grit edges, has got to be done purely on a very personal whim.

I chose 'Inverted V' and 'Right-Hand Buttress' because they were amongst my first leads on grit and both represent good solid value at their respective grades. The former I found almost enjoyable, despite laybacking because I couldn't jam and the latter absolutely terrifying. The techniques employed on Inverted V were not all that different from Lakes climbing but on Right-Hand Buttress there is no escaping the purely gritstone nature. It is climbed on rounded edges up a steep and, in those days, seemingly unprotectable crack.

On the breaking up of the June 1984 Ladies International Meet (organised by the Pinnacle Club) I asked Catherine Destiville and Claudie Dunn (Ducreaux) to ascend these two routes for my camera. Both climbs were damp but they soloed them easily and with obvious delight. At the airport I asked Catherine which area had given, for her, the best and most enjoyable climbing during her visits to Britain.

'The grit,' she replied, 'it is so beautiful.'

Above left: **Claudie Dunn on the typically gritstone crack of Right-Hand Buttress.**
Above: **INVERTED V: 70ft (21m). Very Severe (4b). RIGHT-HAND BUTTRESS: 75ft (23m). Severe (3c).**

NORTHERN ENGLAND: Birch Tree Wall

BIRCH TREE WALL: 50ft (15m). Very Severe.
First Ascent: J. Lees, *circa* 1947.
Location: Brimham Rocks between Harrogate and Pateley Bridge, Yorkshire.
Map Ref: 209637.
Guidebook: *Yorkshire Gritstone* by the Yorkshire Mountaineering Club.

Attitude: Faces west, getting the evening sunshine, but is fairly exposed to the elements.
Rock: Finest Yorkshire gritstone (millstone grit).
Access: Brimham Rocks are situated on the B6165 Knaresborough/Pateley Bridge road, 2 miles (3km) north of Summerbridge and 3 miles (5km) east of Pateley Bridge. From the car park

BIRCH TREE WALL: 50ft (15m). Very Severe.

BIRCH TREE WALL

top wall obscured

crux

T.PAVEY '85

for the rocks walk up the track to the cafe/tourist centre: a path leads down left-wards and round to reach the highest buttress of rock (5 minutes).

Birch Tree Wall – Summary

At the highest part, left-hand side, of the buttress an obvious cleft (Lover's Leap Chimney), topped by huge balanced boulders, splits the rocks. Left again of this Birch Tree Wall follows a series of leftward spiralling grooves and scoops up the steep buttress. Start at the front of the buttress.

1. 50ft (15m), (4c). Gain the groove and up to a ledge on the edge of the buttress. Go left and move up (crux) to below a scoop. Up this to gain a gangway which is followed to the top.

Birch Tree Wall – Description

Situated high above Nidderdale the Brimham Rocks consist of a fantastic collection of stacked pinnacles, with heads bigger than bases, huge blocks and small buttresses. The variety of form and position would not be out of place providing the set for some Western, but situated here, high on a Yorkshire moor and often clothed in mist, the effect is fantastic. Little wonder then, that the rocks were once thought to be the remains of monuments left by the Druids. Their composition of millstone grit, eroded by the effects of wind-blown sand, provides the key to their shape. Unique in Britain, their geology also gives them the qualities revered by the gritstone climber; exceptional friction and savage hand-jamming cracks.

Brimham provides a total gritstone experience. Firstly the atmosphere is much more akin to that of a bigger and wilder mountain environment, where the white silver birch and purple heathers mix with the brown-red grit giving a feeling of softness and seclusion. Secondly there is a fascination of different climbing areas, each with its own microcosm of physical form and climbing technique: The Cubic Block with the famously painful start to Minion's Way (VS) and the jumping trick necessary to succeed on its left-hand neighbour, Joker's Wall (E3); the Walls of The Black Chipper (HVS) and Duggie's Dilemma (S); the backing and footing boldness of Hatters Groove (VS); the beautiful and delectable delicacy of Allan's Slab Direct—one of Allan Austin's little gems; the absolute viciousness of the sardonically named Charming Crack (HVS)—a Joe Brown hand jam special; the isolated Cannon Rock and the unexpected quality of Frensis Direct (HVS).

So how can one choose a route from so many worthy contenders? Well the one that struck me as being something just that little bit more satisfying, just that little bit more challenging perhaps, is named Birch Tree Wall. It is an elegant line and a satisfying climb, the highest on Brimham Rocks.

I think it was the gritstone devotee Dave Cook who described grit as 'leaders rock' and fittingly Birch Tree Wall is a route to be led. On my first visit to the Rocks, a damp autumn,

Wilf Williamson at the crux of Birch Tree Wall.

Above left: **Birch Tree Wall**.
Above right: **Final Groove**.

it stood proudly in resplendent green; greasy, lichenous yet treacherously tempting. Resisting the urge I promptly 'decked out' from some lesser boulders, badly sprained my ankle and was carried off to hospital. But the bug had bitten and I returned early to attempt the elegant line.

The ankle seemed alright for short periods, so long as it wasn't bent sideways, but after only a short while strength alarmingly drained away and pain took over. Would the ankle hold out for the length of Birch Tree Wall? There was only one way to find out.

So with some trepidation I pulled into the first groove and up to the edge of the buttress. There appeared to be a nut crack before the moves left but even though I was tied on to the rope it didn't seem right somehow to place a nut and I made the moves without. They proved balancey and scary and landed me below a rather problematical looking groove.

So far so good, but above the Slab, slanting left seemed to end in a steep wall—could this be the crux at 50ft (15m) with no protection? Well Dave Cook was right; grit is a leader's rock, Birch Tree Wall is a leaders climb, and the ankle, well, I didn't feel it until I floated back to the car.

NORTHERN ENGLAND: Jean Jeanie

JEAN JEANIE: 100ft (30m), (4c). Very Severe.
First Lead: Al Evans *circa* 1970.
Location: Trowbarrow Quarry, near Silverdale, north west Lancashire.
Map Ref: OS 481758.
Guidebook: *Rock Climbs in Lancashire and the North West* by Les Ainsworth.
Attitude: Faces south west and offers all-year-round climbing.
Rock: Fossiliferous, quarried, carboniferous limestone.
Access: The Carnforth (near junction 35 off the M6) to Silverdale road should be followed towards Silverdale station. Immediately before the station (opposite golf course) turn right and

continue past Leighton Moss nature reserve (on right) where the road travels through woods. Just prior to the end of the wood a park can be seen on the left. Follow a muddy track above the road up through the wood until the rim of the quarry is reached. Drop into the quarry and walk along for a further 300 yards (274m) until the obvious Main Wall (10 minutes). *Note:* Although there appears to be no problem with access, the quarry owners—Tarmac—have occasionally requested climbers to leave.

Jean Jeanie – Summary
This takes the striking main wall of the quarry and follows the central most crack. (The

Above left: **Steve Hubbard on the wall of Jean Jeanie.**
Above right: **Moving right.**

JEAN JEANIE

crux

Jean
Jeanie

belay point

**JEAN JEANIE: 100ft (30m), (4c).
Very Severe.**

straightest and most prominent crack—
Aladdin Sane HVS—lies 10ft (3m) to the left.
1. 100ft (30m), 4c. From beneath the crack
pull over to follow the main crack line with a
step right round mid height to the top or,
slightly easier, start right of the crack and
move up leftwards to it.

Jean Jeanie – Description

Trowbarrow Main Wall is a limestone
bedding plane, plastered in fossils, once horizontal, that has been thrown upwards by earth
mechanics to form a nearly vertical wall.
Worked as a quarry, blasting has separated the
face from the main mass of rock behind. The
outward movement cracked the face but left it
still standing, so producing the excellent lines
that are now classic climbs. The whole face is a
bit scary but appears to be mechanically
sound. At the moment holds in the cracks
themselves are good but the fossil holds on the
face tend to fall off! On the whole the climbing
feels reasonably secure, but caution must

always be exercised.

Jean Jeanie is an excellent Very Severe which
although unrelentingly steep for its grade is
reasonable in its execution. Perhaps surprisingly, protection in the crack, a good assort-
ment of nuts, is regular and fairly dependable.

Trowbarrow Quarry is a most unquarry-like
quarry. Open and airy with fine views of the
surrounding countryside, it remains sheltered
and soaks in the sun. Certainly a good venue
for a winter's day, but at its best on a fine
spring evening. All round lies clean air, rich
rolling limestone topography and woods and
fields rich in flowers. If you're early enough in
the season and lucky, you may hear the Bittern
'booming' down on Leighton Moss.

Every year someone says, 'Have you heard,
Trowbarrow Quarry has fallen down—Yeah
the whole face.' But it never has and hopefully,
although possible, it won't do in the near
future.

The routes on the main face are more than
just good climbs for they were done in the
heady times of the early seventies and have

almost a cult following. They were first ascended at a time when new concepts in climbing were being realised and the time when a young lad called Ron Fawcett started to make his mark on the crags. (Aladdin Sane being one of his first new routes.)

Jean Jeanie is a distinguished and enjoyable climb, harder and looser when it was first climbed, but now quite a fair proposition at Very Severe. The definite crux lies above half height, where the crack kinks from left to right, and involves a move which is both delicate and strenuous. Trowbarrow has a lot to offer so in the words of the song 'Jean Jeanie—let yourself go'.

Right: **Up the crack in a sea of fossils.**

NORTHERN ENGLAND: Central Wall and The Thorn (Combination)

CENTRAL WALL AND THE THORN (2nd pitch). 250ft (76m). Very Severe (–, 4b, 4c with 1 pt. of aid).

First Ascent: The Thorn, Joe Brown and Ron Moseley, 1954.
Location: Beeston Tor in the Manifold Valley, Staffordshire Area, Peak District National Park (nearest large town, Buxton).
Map Ref: 106541.
Guidebooks: *Staffordshire Area* by British Mountaineering Council. *Rock Climbing in the Peak District* by Paul Nunn.
Attitude: Faces south and is very sheltered—can be climbed comfortably even when there is deep snow on the ground.
Altitude: 700ft (213m).
Rock: Pocketed limestone.
Access: From the A515 Buxton to Ashbourne road, drive through Alstonfield to Wetton. From here follow the Grindon and Manifold road down a series of hairpin bends to Weags Bridge. Immediately fork left (dust road) down to a farm. Cars may be parked in a field just before the farm on payment of a small fee to the farmer (excellent value). Cross the river via stepping stones and up to the crag via a muddy path (3 minutes).

Central Wall and The Thorn (last pitch) – Summary

The feature of the climb is the distinct sandwiched slab, giving access to the huge cave of Ivy Gash, lying on the steep central wall of the crag. Thorn then breaks out steeply from the left-hand end of the Ivy Gash. Start below the clean wall where a streak through the vegetated lower rocks can be gained from the muddy path traverse below.

1. 60ft (18m). Follow the runnel worn through the foliage to two in situ peg belays.

2. 90ft (27m), (4b). Up the wall, working diagonally leftwards to the obvious gangway slab. Follow this with a step left at the top to gain Ivy Gash. Thread belay.

3. 30ft (9m). Move down Ivy Gash passing the chain thread abseil point to a small ledge and two, very large, thread belays. (Thorn belay.)

4. 70ft (21m), (4c with 1 piton for aid—5a without). Step down and out leftwards. Steeply follow the arete to an overlap, peg for aid, move up to reach good holds in the base of the groove on the left (peg runners in situ). Follow the groove then step left and follow the rib to move through bushes to ledge and tree belays.

Tim Valley at the crux of The Thorn.

Central Wall and The Thorn – Description

I have chosen a combination of routes here which includes Central Wall in its entirety and then takes the second and best pitch of The Thorn, the reason being that Central Wall gains the large cave (Ivy Gash) and then abseils back down to the ground from an abseil point within a few feet of the belay on The Thorn. Although The Thorn is somewhat harder than Central Wall, if the in situ piton is used for aid (as it was climbed originally) the standard becomes compatible with that of Central Wall. The combination therefore gives a logical and superb way up the cliff.

Beeston Tor is hidden snugly in the Manifold Valley and faces south. A real suntrap, it's almost always warm and dry even in midwinter. In fact for hay fever sufferers and those intolerant of rich limestone flora (jungle) it is best climbed upon in winter. The crag has character as does the climbing; the limestone being extensively endowed with solution pockets which, invisible from below, give splendid incut holds.

The first pitch of Central Wall resembles a garden path, in summer, with luxuriant vegetation towering over you on each side. But by the time the belay below the second pitch is reached the attractions of the climb become apparent. Above you soars the elegant indented gangway, the striking feature of this wall as seen from below.

From the two good in situ piton belays the quality of the rock and the pockets immediately make amends for the overgrown rocks below. Enjoyable climbing with increasingly good position leads, all too quickly, to an awkward move left and a few steps up to gain the cave. Here a good thread belay can be found.

The feeling in the ivy-draped cave is one of being in some jungle retreat, with the security of the limestone almost hugging you in position, but the vertical wall below, the sloping nature of the floor and the shout of your second quickly bring back reality.

Down the sloping ramp that forms the floor of Ivy Gash a chain can be seen, securely threaded round a large limestone column. A few feet below this another two enormous threads can be made and this is the belay for 'The Thorn'.

Move down the chimney then pull out leftwards onto the imposing limestone pillar. The climbing is very steep but the holds are good. Where the rock steps out in a little overhang there is an in situ piton (three in total on the pitch) and if this is used for aid the climbing stays at reasonable Very Severe. If

not the moves are strenuous and a long reach left is required to gain good holds again. Soon it is possible to rest and then the climbing continues at a steady standard up a little

John Thorpe on the ramp of Central Wall.

CENTRAL WALL,
THE THORN

Ivy Gash

The Thorn

Central
Wall

O belay point

Moving up the ramp on Central
Wall, fingers in pockets.

CENTRAL WALL AND THE THORN (2nd pitch): 250ft (76m). Very Severe (-, 4b, 4c with 1pt of aid).

groove to a rib and then the top. A comfortable ledge and stout tree belays mark the end of a notable climb.

This combination of routes gives you a taste of the best steep limestone climbing, but on good holds and at a steady and reasonable grade. Indeed, position and quality of climbing made this into a bit of Derbyshire limestone to savour.

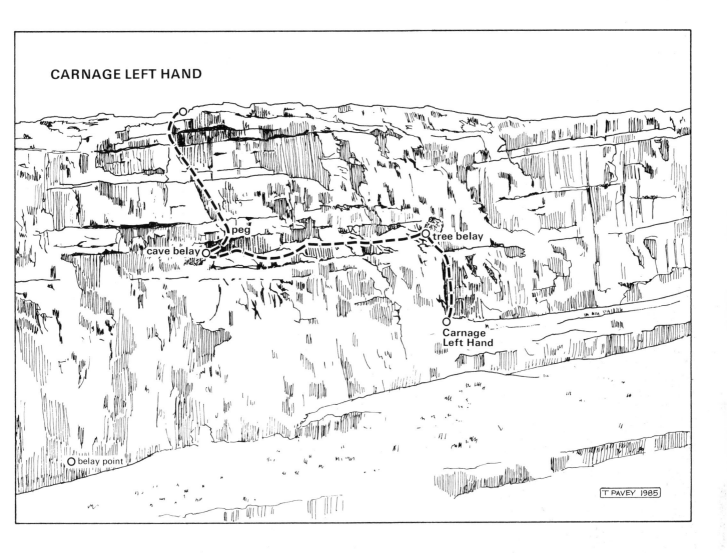

CARNAGE LEFT HAND

cave belay • peg • tree belay

Carnage Left Hand

belay point

T PAVEY 1985

NORTHERN ENGLAND: Carnage Left Hand

CARNAGE LEFT HAND: 200ft (60m).
Extremely Severe E1 (5a, 5a, 5b).
First Ascent: Tony Barley, Robin Barley, *circa* mid 1960s.
Location: Right wing of Malham Cove lies ³/₄ mile above (north) of Malham village in the Yorkshire Dales National Park.
Map Ref: SD 897642.
Guidebook: *Yorkshire Limestone* by the Yorkshire Mountaineering Club.
Attitude: Faces south, forms a suntrap and dries quickly.
Rock: Limestone, generally good.
Access: Malham Cove is easily accessible from either Malham village where there is a huge car park associated with the National Park Centre or from the road which leads towards Malham Tarn on the east of the village, where a widening gives parking and a signposted stile leads to the top of the Cove (10 minutes).

Carnage Left Hand – Summary

On the right of centre lies a square buttress of rock. Immediately after this the wall is halved in size by the grassy terrace. Start on the left end of the terrace at an obvious little corner. The climb takes this to the grass/tree ledge then follows the distinct horizontal break to a cave stance from which a peg move enables a steep diagonal slash above the cave to be reached.

1. 40ft (12m), (5a). Up the deceptively difficult corner to a little tree then left and up again to ledge and tree belay.

2. 90ft (27m), (5a). Move down and left to the last tree before the wall becomes unbroken. Step back up (keeping low is much harder) and traverse leftwards, with a move downwards, near the ledge, to reach a cave stance.

CARNAGE LEFT HAND: 200ft (60m). **Extremely Severe E1 (5a, 5a, 5b).**

3. 70ft (21m), (5b). Move left a few feet to the first peg in the roof and use this to pull over onto the vertical wall above (goes free at 6b). Move up to a horizontal crack then left to the corner. Climb this steeply to the overhangs then step left and up easily to a variety of small belays.

Carnage Left Hand – Description

Malham is the showpiece of Yorkshire limestone climbing. This natural rock amphitheatre, with its great 300-ft (91m) high central wall, teems with horizontal overhangs and sobering verticality. Its striking white and black presents a surprisingly good variety of climbs and invariably it reflects the day's sunshine and laughs at showers of rain. After prolonged rain, however, it begins unhappily to weep and drip and should be left a number of days to cheer up.

Every summer weekend throngs of tourists methodically file beneath it, gaze in awe, split and scrabble up its left and right flanks. Invariably they totter across the polished leg-snapping grikes of the limestone pavement above and meet at the snout. After shuddering, exchanging pleasantries regarding the splashes of colour they have observed scaling the walls, they return, scrabbling down the opposite flank.

The kids throw paper aeroplanes from the top, or practise for the Yorkshire Eleven in the meadows below or even, the unruly ones, scramble on the rock walls themselves.

Until recently the wings of Malham were the province of the free rock climber and the central walls and overhangs belonged to the aid climber—the 'bang-and-wallop' brigade who would swing methodically from expansion bolt to expansion bolt, speedily ascending the apparently blank walls. Today much of this central wall area is 'free climbed' at an impressively high technical standard.

On the wings the difficulties are not so great, and the lines and natural features better defined. Carnage Left Hand is such a route giving a climb of good length, high exposure and sound quality. It starts apparently innocuously up a rather insignificant-looking corner.

A few moves soon bring home the true difficulty of the pitch and the uncompromising steepness of the limestone. From the sheltered tree ledge the exposure hits you hard and immediately it overhangs above and is straight vertical below, yet your position seems to stick out somehow and beneath your feet there seems to be only space. The third time I did it my partner got lost and went low, with apparently no effort and no runners. With sweating palms, rubber fingers and bulging eyes I attempted to follow, only my mind couldn't equate the difficulty with the supposed grade. I'd never had this bother before and I retreated back right feeling embarrassed by my ineptitude. Wilf (my partner) and the world looked on smiling inwardly.

I felt pathetic—perhaps it was really time to pack in this crazy game. Wilf's shouts confirmed my thoughts. Hang it—there has got to be something wrong with that line—HVS no way, I thought. Then it dawned, a step up and things thankfully flowed again.

The stance is comfortable and it takes effort to swing into space on the rusty old peg above the roof, but once committed you're forced to keep moving—hoping the steep wall will be kind. It is and the climbing, typically limestone, rewards the bold approach. Both position and climbing are magnificent and it's funny but all the time you're on that limestone wall you don't hear the crowd, see the paper aeroplanes or care if the Yorkshire Eleven are batting or bowling.

Far left: Wilf Williamson traversing the second pitch of Carnage Left Hand.
Right: **High on the wall.**

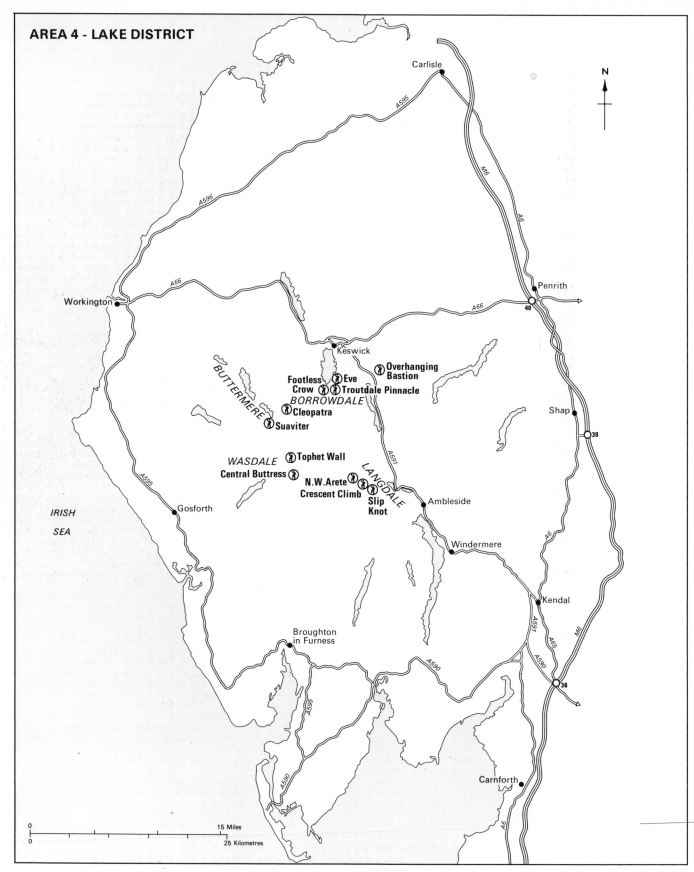

AREA 4 - LAKE DISTRICT

N

Carlisle

Workington

Penrith

40

Keswick

Overhanging
Bastion

Footless Eve
Crow Troutdale Pinnacle

BORROWDALE

Cleopatra

Suaviter

Shap

39

Tophet Wall

WASDALE

Central Buttress

N.W. Arete

Crescent Climb

Slip
Knot

LANGDALE

Ambleside

Windermere

Gosforth

IRISH

SEA

Broughton
in Furness

Kendal

Carnforth

0
0
15 Miles
25 Kilometres

THE LAKE DISTRICT: Crescent Climb and Gwynne's Chimney (Combination)

CRESCENT CLIMB: 330ft (100m). Moderate.
First Ascent: F. Botterill, W.E. Palmer, 1907.
GWYNNE'S CHIMNEY: 80ft (24m). Difficult.
First Ascent: H.A. Gwynne and party, 1892.
Location: Pavey Ark, Great Langdale, Lake District.
Map Ref: 286080.
Guidebooks: *Rock Climbing in the Lake District* by Cram, Eilbeck, Roper, *Great Langdale* (F&RCC Guide) by M.G. Mortimer.
Attitude: Faces south.

Altitude: 1,700ft (518m).
Rock: Rhyolite (vegetated below Jack's Rake—better above).
Access: From the New Dungeon Ghyll go directly up to Stickle Tarn. Crag is best reached by walking on left side of Tarn (40 minutes).
Descent: Down Jack's Rake—obvious diagonal rake crossing the crag, or down east gully on right side (east) of crag.
STONEFALL: Beware of stonefall from Jack's Rake.

Pavey Ark with Stickle Tarn in the foreground.

Crescent Climb – Summary

Near the centre of the crag to the right of the obvious gullies and just right of a large buttress (Stony Buttress) there is a vegetated blind gully with a broken ridge on its right. Directly above, the most obvious feature from Stickle Tarn, is the distinctive crescent. Start at foot of gully.

1. 180ft. (55m). Climb the ridge until good belays can be eventually reached at the start of the crescent traverse.

2. 50ft (15m). Traverse right under overhang.

3. 100ft (30m). Ascend broken rocks then grass to reach Jack's Rake.

Continue up.

Gwynne's Chimney – Summary

Starts just over on the right, immediately above Jack's Rake.

1. 5ft (16m). Up the chimney, using various techniques, to belay on a small but stout Yew tree.

2. 5ft (8m). Either continue up the chimney—usually wet, very restrictive and never pleasant—*or* move right and climb the airy rib on small, bubbly holds. The rock is delightfully rough.

Afterwards it is usual to unrope and scramble up the obvious trod, via various rocky sections, to reach the summit of Pavey Ark.

Crescent Climb and Gwynne's Chimney – Description

Any route associated with the character Fred Botterill has got to be worthy of consideration and the Crescent Climb combined with Gwynne's Chimney give a purposeful mountaineering route right to the summit of Pavey Ark. From the dam which holds back Stickle Tarn the Crescent is one of the most obvious features of the front face of the huge rambling and vegetated Pavey Ark. At this distance it looks formidable, but only on closer acquaintance does its true character become known.

Rather broken and vegetated in its execution, it is nevertheless worthily situated and noticeably exposed. The extent and degree of difficulty of the traverse under the Crescent being indeterminable until one actually embarks upon it. It looks, with overhangs above and slabs steepening rapidly into a large wall below, as though it cannot possibly be anything but hard. When you actually get to grips with it, amazingly, you could, as they say locally, 'Drive a horse and cart across it'. But, perhaps illogically, this only serves to enhance the character of the route.

George Basterfield in the first F&RCC 'Red' Series Guide, gave it a wonderfully descriptive introduction—guaranteed to put off any prospective rock climbers!

'This climb is recommended for the summer time,

CRESCENT CLIMB: 330ft (100m). Moderate. GWYNNE'S CHIMNEY: 80ft (24m). Difficult.

CRESCENT CLIMB AND GWYNNE'S CHIMNEY

Gwynne's Chimney

Jack's Rake

The Crescent

O belay point

and to climbing botanists. It is delightfully fragrant, and but for 50 feet of traverse, the whole route is redolent with the perfume of a wild riot of blossoming vegetation. One can pause frequently to inhale at leisure the sweet aroma and feast the eyes on the rich hues of this hanging garden of nature, a scene of rampant anarchy.'

And he continued, commenting on Gwynne's Chimney thus:

'Usually taken in conjunction with the Crescent Climb, as a compensating rock finish to the summit of the crag.'

Despite the underlying truth in these words, even today when undoubtedly the rocks are somewhat cleaner, both routes do have an endearing quality, making their combination into a recommendable expedition. Specifically, it's hard to say why, but I think one factor is just that, that they are easy and pleasant. Flowers en route, no great technical difficulty, but fine exposure, does make a very pleasing change to the shiny, monotonous nature of so many early rock climbs. Gwynne's Chimney in its turn complements and contrasts with Crescent Climb. A typical chimney of the classic school, it gives all rock climbing, requiring a number of techniques.

Pavey Ark is deceptively large, initially appearing to be wholly vegetation and unworthy of the rock climber's attention. On closer scrutiny, however, there is plenty of rock tucked away, simply dwarfed by the 500-ft (152m) high mass of crag. Above Jack's Rake, the tourist scramble up the crag and a useful means of descent for the climber, the rock is wonderfully rough and bubbly—some of the roughest rock in Lakeland. Below the nature is different and the rocks tend to be smoother, more flakey, much less reliable (lumps and spikes often pull off) and liberally splattered with vegetation.

It's on this latter terrain that Crescent Climb kicks off up a broken rib, where in true mountaineering tradition, climbing together is

Below left: **Susan Lund chimneying.**
Below right: **The bubbly wall.**

necessitated by the absence of a reliable belay. It soon feels quite exposed. On the left lies a gully and the huge domineering wall of Stony Buttress and to the right a further steep wall and the climbing can be enjoyed for the exposure alone.

Of some note may be the fact that you are now situated between two climbs which were once the subject of notorious controversies and a subject of some correspondence at the time (mid 1970s). On the left lies Pete Livesey's and Barry Rogers' Sally Free 'N' Easy or was it Rod Valentine's and Allan Austin's Ragman's Trumpet. It seemed a matter of some contention, each party claiming they climbed the wall first! The latter party, being the guide-writers, had the winning hand at the time. Over on the right lies Cruel Sister, now one of the mode popular climbs of Extreme grade (E3) in the valley, but at the time dismissed by the same guide-writers as unacceptable due to its mode of ascent. For the climber on Crescent Climb it doesn't really seem to matter at all; other factors such as whether the sun's shining, or if the hold about to be used is acceptably safe, taking proper precedence.

Wonderfully easy, the traverse is an excellent pitch on which to initiate the beginner. There are good belays on either side and bucket holds with big exposure gives a great feeling of elation to those taking their first steps. Afterwards it becomes a mere walk up steep grass to reach the, usually popular, well-worn path of Jack's Rake.

Over on the right, Gwynne's Chimney is a distinct rectangular weakness above the Rake. The climbing in the chimney is on good sound rock and utilises all the techniques associated with chimneying. Those of jamming, knees, backing and footing and bridging to mention only a few. Originally one of the main features, The Gun, offered a helping handhold up the most awkward section, but this has subsequently disappeared!

From the comfortable belay round the yew I prefer to step right and climb the rib. The holds are small, but very good, and though steep one can remain in balance. It's a delightfully airy finish to rather a nice little chimney climb. Afterwards it is usual to discard the rope, although care should be taken for it's a long way down! Scrambling remains to the summit of Pavey Ark, a magnificent view and an excellent situation to eat one's sandwiches.

The Crescent Climb/Gwynne's Chimney combination gives a very worthwhile ascent of a mountain crag. It's particularly well suited to 'blood' a beginner (and has drawn real blood) but shouldn't be merely written off as a climb solely for the novice as it has a number of virtues worthy of consideration. For those wanting a quiet day climbing a large face to the summit of a mountain, or perhaps, for the practised, a solo day out, or as a climb to be done in any conditions, there can be few more enjoyable courses.

You don't even have to be a qualified botanist—a keen amateur in the party will serve equally well!

THE LAKE DISTRICT: Troutdale Pinnacle (Black Crag Buttress)

TROUTDALE PINNACLE: 370ft (113m). Severe (Mild).
First Ascent: F. Mallinson and R. Mayson, 4 May 1914.
Location: Black Crag, Borrowdale, Lake District.
Map Ref: 263174.
Guidebooks: *Rock Climbing in the Lake District* by Birkett, Cram, Eilbeck and Roper. *Borrowdale* (F&RCC Guide) by D. Armstrong and R. Kenyon.
Attitude: Faces north west.
Altitude: 800ft (244m).
Rock: Borrowdale Volanics.
Access: Up the Borrowdale road from Keswick (3½ miles, 5km) past the Borrowdale Hotel (on left) and before the Grange Bridge (on right) a right-angled bend has Derwent View House on the right and the track leading to Black Crag on the left. Just past the bend, on the left, there is a purpose-made car park. Follow the track to a gate and on through the field of Troutdale (Old Trout ponds over on left) until one can break left over the stream and climb directly through the woods to the bottom of the crag (20 minutes).
Descent: Up towards top of hill and then follow a well-worn little path (on right) leading across and down, in a rock slab, to footpath traversing beneath crag.

Troutdale Pinnacle – Summary

Start at the very toe of the rocks, where the footpath arrives.

1. 35ft (11m). The steep thrutchy crack or the chimney on the left lead to a ledge. Belay on tree on the right.

2. 45ft (14m). Step up left onto the wall, and continue to a rock pinnacle belay.

3. 95ft (29m). Climb the groove on the right to gain access to a slab slanting up rightwards to another natural jammed rock pinnacle. (Thread belay).

4. 35ft (11m). Move right into the steep corner and up that until it is possible to move up and left to small stance and belays (thread) on the edge of the main slab.

5. 70ft (21m). Traverse the slabs leftwards beneath the overhangs until a step down places you below a short bulging wall. Climb up leftwards to gain a rock ledge.

6. 45ft (14m). Straight up to the crest of the pinnacle. The corner on the right is easiest, a

groove directly above hardest.

7. 45ft (14m). Gain the groove on the edge

Pitch three on Troutdale Pinnacle with Derwentwater in the background.

TROUTDALE PINNACLE

The Pinnacle

crux   slab

belay point

→

**TROUTDALE PINNACLE: 370ft
(113m). Severe (Mild).**

above and steeply up this moving right and then pulling leftwards through overhanging rock near the top. Continue to belay well back on the ledge.

Troutdale Pinnacle –
Description

When Troutdale Pinnacle was first put up in 1914 by two local men from Keswick—F. Mallinson and R. Mayson (photographer)—it was one of only, literally, a handful of rock climbs in Borrowdale. Ralph Mayson wrote of his climb:

'A new climb has this season been discovered in the interesting rock areas nearer Keswick. It is the cliff at the head of Troutdale, opposite Mouse Ghyll on the other side of the valley. It starts easily but increases in difficulty, the situations on the upper reaches are sensational, the finish is stiff, and the Troutdale Pinnacle, as it will probably be called, furnishes 250ft. or 280ft. of first-rate climbing.' (F&RCC Journal 1914-15, Vol. 3, No. 2).

Despite this Borrowdale was virtually ig-. nored in favour of the already well-established

climbing areas around Wasdale and even over a decade later in the first climbers' guide to the valley (*Great Gable and Borrowdale*—FRCC Guide) A. R. Thompson described the climbs as few and far between.

How times change, for Borrowdale is now swamped by both climbs and climbers. Yet of the myriad of climbs below the Very Severe category I cannot think of a better all-round climb than Mallinson and Mayson's Troutdale Pinnacle. It may well be polished, but the rock is sound and clean, and the climbing very good, varied, even sensational. Another attraction is its location. Situated in a charming and pleasant little spur off the main Borrowdale valley, only a mere 15 minutes' stroll from the car, it is a subtle and contrasting environment to the higher fiercer mountain crags.

I suppose Borrowdale is now the strawberries and cream, or even the Wimbledon, of Lakeland climbing and this is reflected by the numbers of attendant climbers. But one shouldn't be put off by this. It is unarguably a different world to the great north-facing

Scafell Crag or even the pure rock scenery of White Ghyll (Langdale) yet it exhibits charm and lightness that is irresistibly appealing. Quite apart from the ice-creams, cafes and pubs which abound in nearby Keswick, the valley itself is probably the most beautiful of all the Lakeland valleys (difficult to measure). Take a look down Derwentwater from above Ashness Bridge, on the Watendlath road, on a fine summer's day or a quiet autumn afternoon, or perhaps when the snow has whitened the top of Skiddaw—and then the colours, the juxtaposition of the water, the islands, the wood and fells will take your breath away. It could be Switzerland, the Japanese Alps or New Hampshire, but there again, not really, for it has a quaintness of scale that is, on consideration, unique.

Surrounded by trees, Black Crag is much bigger than it appears and despite the multitude of routes and variations teeming up virtually every square inch of rock, Troutdale Pinnacle remains, simple and obvious—*the* route of the crag. Starting at the lowest point, it gains a slanting slab system leading rightwards to beneath the largest overhangs then breaking left across a great slab to steeper ground and the top of the ultimately exposed pinnacle. A 40-ft (12-m) crest gives a very steep and airy finish to a superb and contrasting rock climb.

The last time I climbed the route was one of those fortunate occasions when the day begins damp and disheartening to suddenly and unexpectedly blossom into sunshine and summer heat.

We started out with legs soaked from brushing wet bracken and with trees dripping on to our heads from the very bottom of the buttress, and finished, amidst blue skies, at the highest point of the crag.

Initially things weren't too pleasant with slime and mud making the opening chimney a bit of a fight, but by the time we reached the rock pinnacle belay of the second pitch, the rocks were drying out rapidly. From this point the route takes off as a climb and the next long pitch is both steeper and harder. All rock now, the increasing altitude begins to make itself felt and another good belay in the form of a thread round a large, if somewhat detached, rock needle is very welcome.

The next section is very polished; a short bulging corner groove, at the limit of the grade, leads trickily to a small stance on the edge of the big slab breaking leftwards beneath the overhangs. Crossing the slab requires a cool approach and involves a neat two-step movement to descend into a corner to stand beneath a short, slightly overhanging and

Left: **On the pinnacle.**

Below: **Looking down to the pinnacle.**

Above left: **Susan Lund starting the big slab traverse**.
Above right: **The final groove**.

distinctly awkward-looking wall. This is the crux and it was running with water.

I found it awkward and difficult, wide bridging on small holds in a vain attempt to keep my feet on dry rock. But most of all I remember it being extremely strenuous, involving long reaches and ultimately a desperate pinch on a pathetically wet hold.

The traverse was a mixture, the slabby rock was dry but all the incut holds, of which fortunately there is an ample supply, held the water in pools. On taking in the rope I pulled out my only runner, which was placed just after the worst bit of the long descending traverse beneath the overhangs. It is very obvious from the stance that the second, in these circumstances, is in a much more serious position than the leader. A fall from the traverse would result in unthinkable consequences.

Back on the previous belay at the edge of the great slab, I was belaying on a long sling which I had, at the foot of the climb, given to Susan Lund, my second, and asked her to untie a footloop knot. This had enabled the sling to be used for jumarring on some earlier escapade. She did this and handed it back. I gave the belay a second glance and somehow it didn't look quite right. The ends of the sling were still taped securely back, but there didn't appear to be a knot holding it together, only a curious

kink in the body of the sling. I gave it a yank and the ends of the sling divided, the tape broke, and the belay hung limp in my hand! 'Well you asked me to undo the knot,' she beseeched. In fact, logically enough for the inexperienced, she had undone the footloop knot and loosened, into the body of the sling, the knot tying the sling together. I was now growing in concern as to how Susan was going to perform on the descending traverse, where one slip would be serious. She, of course, bombed it!

If a little groove is followed directly, the next section of climbing, to gain the top of the pinnacle, is quite demanding although there is an easier variation to the right. The top of the pinnacle gives that feeling of absolute exposure that the novice dreams about. A thumb of rock, near the top of the crag, sticking out 200ft (60m) or more above the foot of the climb.

Rising vertically above the knife-edge ridge leading to the pinnacle, the final arete soars handsomely to the top of the crag. And what a pitch; it feels like the steepest part of the route; overhangs sprout above your head and it needs a thoughtful and plucky approach to succeed. A fitting end to a route that offers almost 400ft (122m) of solid rock climbing. Anyone for Borrowdale?

THE LAKE DISTRICT: Suaviter, Oxford and Cambridge Direct Route (Combination)

SUAVITER: 135ft (41m). Severe.
First Ascent: W. Peascod and S.B. Beck, 12 July 1941.
OXFORD AND CAMBRIDGE DIRECT ROUTE: 125ft (38m). Severe.
First Ascent: H.V. Reade, September 1914.
Location: Grey Crag, Birkness Combe, High Stileface, Buttermere, Lake District.
Map Ref: 172148.
Guidebooks: *Rock Climbing in the Lake District* by Birkett, Cram, Eilbeck, Roper, *Buttermere and Eastern Crags* (F&RCC Guide) by I.

Roper.
Attitude: Faces south east.
Altitude: 2,250ft (685m).
Rock: Hard and rough rhyolite.
Access: Grey Crags lie at the top right, High Stile side, of Birkness Combe. Walk from Gatesgarth farm, first following a track across level fields and then breaking rightwards up the fell. (1 hour).
Descent: Best left of Oxford and Cambridge then right of Suaviter. (Facing in.)

Birkness Combe above Buttermere.

Oxford and
Cambridge
Direct

Suaviter

○ belay point

**SUAVITER: 135ft (41m). Severe.
OXFORD AND CAMBRIDGE
DIRECT ROUTE: 125ft (38m).
Severe.**

Suaviter – Summary

If one imagines the layout of Grey Crag to be roughly triangular, then Suaviter lies on the buttress which forms the bottom-right of the triangle and Oxford and Cambridge Buttress lies above (it is the highest crag) forming the apex of the triangle.

The line takes an attractive thin crack up the clean Slab Wall on the left side of the buttress. Start by a boulder below a wide chimney/crack.

1. 20ft (6m). Up the chimney through the overlap (quite awkward) to gain the rock ledge and flake belays. (The Balcony.)

2. 50ft (15m). Move down left and traverse until a step up can be made to gain the thin crack in the middle of the wall. Up, passing loose blocks at the top, to belay on a corner ledge on the left.

3. 65ft (20m). Continue straight up, finally following a chimney to the top.

It is now attractive to wander across to the upper Buttress to where Oxford and Cambridge Direct follows the extreme left arete/corner of the clean wall.

Oxford and Cambridge Direct Route – Summary

Start immediately right of the arete.

1. 45ft (14m). Move up to gain the arete, climb to its left then regain the edge, following this to ledge and thread belay.

2. 80ft (24m). Climb the bulging crack on the left, then move back right to the arete. Follow the edge directly to the top (exposed and balancy).

Suaviter, Oxford and Cambridge Direct Route (Combination) – Description

The Buttermere Valley remains the quietest side of Lakeland. Its expressions are pastel: the lake green, the crags grey and every autumn the brackens, shooting up to Birkness Combe, show their burnt red. One feels no compulsion to hurry here for the climber setting off through the Gatesgarth farm yard has a range of routes and crags from which to choose. A short, though excessively steep, haul brings High Crag to hand, or a little further on and up into Birkness Combe—Eagle Crag. If this is wet, invariably black, or, perhaps, occupied, then take a stroll across the screes to Grey Crag on High Stile.

Suaviter and Oxford and Cambridge Direct Route are chosen to fit into this relaxed and rather gentle atmosphere, although there are two qualities which go some way to belie this: their steepness and the immediacy of exposure felt. However, these factors are more than compensated for by their sunny disposition and the liberal nature of the holds. Even on a winter's day the crag can be bathed in sunshine and the rock (being both rough and sound) is the finest to be found in Buttermere.

The secret delights of Buttermere have been discovered, only to be forgotten on a number of occasions. A.R. Thompson (*circa* 1927) had written in the first true published Guidebook (F&RCC—*Rock Climbing in Buttermere*):

'Buttermere as a climbing centre is distinguished by its wet gullies. These contain, besides water, much loose material, and must all be approached with caution. Since Oppenheimer's 'Heart of Lakeland', written about sixteen years ago, the only great discovery has been the possibilities of increased climbing in Birkness Coombe. In wet weather, indeed in all weathers, it claims first attention. There only are to be found the face climbs on good hard rock, which give satisfaction to the modern climber.'

It was during this period that H.V. Reade climbed Oxford and Cambridge Direct Route, but our other route, Suaviter wasn't climbed until the time immediately preceding the following words written by C.W.F. Noyce (*Buttermere*—'And Boat Howe', 1942, Journal of F&RCC);

'Buttermere, if you look for them, has most of the climbing amenities.
– Take Grey Crags on High Stile, for they are airiest and most inviting of all, sun splashed and restful. Here I found, are fine possibilities of gym-shoe wandering.
– Too much of Grey Crags after army diet is like champagne on indigestion.'

This latter route was led by Bill Peascod, the miner, and named by Bert Beck, the scholar. A powerful team producing an aptly named climb—their last before Beck was sent off to War. In two summers these two did more for Buttermere climbing than anyone before or since.

It is worth noting their, now classic, sequence of first ascents done in this short space of time. Far East Buttress (VS), Border Buttress (VS), Eagle Girdle (VS), Eagle Front (VS), Fifth Avenue (VS), Dexter Wall (VS), The Y Gully (VS), Fortiter (VS) and finally Suaviter (S). All, with the exception of Suaviter, in the Very Severe category. Interestingly, neither of the pair had ever climbed a

guidebook-rated VS—they just felt, intuitively, that their routes must be VS.

With the above pedigree Suaviter promises much and, although short, it has a distinctive charm so typical of Grey Crags. To reach what Peascod named 'The Balcony', an attractive rock ledge where one can view both the climb and the scenery, there are two starts. The obvious one climbs directly up a little chimney groove and is awkward enough to make you think (slightly left is supposedly easier). But it is only from here on that Suaviter earns its name. The object now is the thin crack in the middle of the grey slab. To reach it requires a degree of composure for the position is most definitely airy.

Holds are good, square cut and rough for both hands and feet, but one must think to fit them together. After the traverse, when the crack is reached, one should try to ignore the obvious and plentiful nut placements, so to preserve the original thrill of the climb. At the top of this pitch some sizeable loose blocks should be treated with respect. Really the rocks above don't offer much interest, but the route has already been more than justified by that one absolutely delectable pitch.

Stroll easily over to the top crag. The clean cracked wall is taken by Dexter Wall (VS) a route which has a technical and bold crux

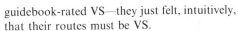

Above left: **John Hargreaves on the edge.**
Above right: **Over the bulge.**

Above left: **Brenda Wilkinson at the first pitch on Suaviter.**
Above right: **John Hargreaves on the bold slab.**

should you wish to try it. On its left Oxford and Cambridge Direct Route more or less follows the arete. It doesn't look much, rather ragged and seems to step back at an easy angle.

However, appearances can be deceptive. It is in fact steep and exposed. After a few feet, when the crest is gained, the technicalities suddenly appear. Most step left and up the side before regaining the edge. Soon a substantial rock ledge is reached, situated below a steep little wall.

This obstacle is passed by climbing an overhanging fist-wide crack on the left. Now you traverse right and from here on, the climb sticks purely to the edge. It's both steep and precariously exposed. Protection takes the form of a tape sling and its distance from the bulging crux makes it a lonely lead. But have

faith in what may be above, the holds are incut and of ample size.

Both these routes have great character and if Severe is the hardest grade you've ever led then you'll feel wonderfully elated on reaching the top. Come to think of it, even if you have led climbs graded considerably harder, that same feeling will still be there. For these two little climbs have a quality that transcends mere technical difficulty—in fact they contain the essence of a really classic day in the mountains.

The truth is that Buttermere has never really been hot climbing news. Neither has it ever been regarded as the 'in' centre of rock climbing development. Selfishly, I'm rather pleased—Cinderella without her glass slipper seems to me more appealing.

THE LAKE DISTRICT: Tophet Wall

TOPHET WALL: 265ft (81m). (Severe).
First Ascent: H.M. Kelly and R.E.W. Pritchard, 1923.
Location: Tophet Wall, The Napes area of Great Gable, Lake District.
Map Ref: 211099.
Guidebooks: *Rock Climbing in the Lake District* by Cram, Eilbeck, Roper. *Great Gable* (F&RCC Guide) by P.L. Fearnehough.
Attitude: Faces south east.
Altitude: 2,500ft (762m).
Rock: Rhyolite with excellent flake holds.
Access: Either approach from Borrowdale via the Sty Head Pass (one hour) or more traditionally and more quickly from Wasdale via the other end of Sty Head Pass. Both arrive at the Col above Sty Head Tarn from where the Gable traverse path contours round the south-west Face of the mountain, first underneath the clean and distinctive Kern Knotts Crag then

underneath a large scree and boulder-strewn gully above which stretches the large clean Tophet Wall. Better to go a little further along the path and approach the Wall via a path coming in from the left.
Descent: Down the large scree shoot on the right; Great Hell Gate.

Tophet Wall – Summary

Start in the centre of the crag just right of a distinctive overhanging corner crack.

1. 85ft (26m). Go up the wall right of the crack, then move across left into the crack. Climb it to a ledge then continue rightwards up the ramp to a grass ledge below the steep wall (original route traversed in from the right at this point).

2. 55ft (17m). Straight up the wall to ledge then left to large open corner. Up the crack

then the right wall to belay in the top right of the corner.

3. 50ft (15m). The obvious horizontal traverse rightwards. At the end climb the rib right of the corner to a stance.

4. 75ft (23m). Up the pinnacle then the

crack on the left to gain a rock ledge (30ft, 9m). Scrambling leads in a further 45ft (14m) to the top of the ridge.

Just ahead an easy gully drops rightwards into Great Hell Gate.

Tophet Wall – Description

It is not always easy to detail the particular blend of qualities that make a single route into a rock climb of distinction and, in point of fact, it may well be impossible, for what is attractive to one may obviously be less appealing to another. Some of the virtues of Tophet Wall are there for all to see, it is obviously an excellent line up a splendidly clean and largely overhanging buttress of rock, and no climber could fail to appreciate this. Yet, for me, it is some of its hidden qualities, those only discovered by climbing it, that make it into one of the most magnificent rock climbs, of its grade, in Britain.

In general there is a particular quality to Lakeland climbing, a facet which isn't often captured to the same degree elsewhere. Certainly Cumbrian Crags would be dwarfed if compared in stature to the average Scottish cliff and in turn many Lakeland routes appear dull when compared to the exciting naked boldness of many Welsh lines, yet when climbed, the intricacies and concentration of the technicalities of a Lakeland route often prove to be unsurpassable. They have been described as jewels, small but bright and captivating and, in this context, Tophet Wall would take pride of place on any diamond tiara.

Harry Kelly, although schooled on gritstone, was bitten by the Lakeland bug. He wrote,

'My first real climbing holiday in the Lakes was at Great Langdale at Easter 1916, although I had visited Wasdale at Christmas 1914. Until 1922 my holidays were roughly divided between Wales and the Lake District. I preferred the latter for longer spells and began to think that there was no place like Wasdale Head. I lost my heart to it so that when Morley Wood tried to inveigle me back to Wales by talking about 'a mighty unclimbed cliff' called Clogwyn du'r Arddu, I am afraid that I turned a deaf ear to his entreaties!'

Kelly produced a number of excellent routes, Tophet Wall being one of the finest. It did not succumb easily and he along with R.E.W. Pritchard, attempted the problem on a number of occasions.

The first of these was on the 30 August 1920 and it wasn't until 14 July 1923 that he eventually succeeded. But what better adventure to while away the hot summer days than bathed in the shade of this spectacular and,

TOPHET WALL: 265ft (81m). Severe.

TOPHET WALL

Mark Greenbank

Tony Greenbank

○ belay point

then, virgin bastion of rock. After the first ascent he recorded in his diary the following comment:

'I forgot to mention that G just got up from Hell Gate to see me finish off the climb and had thoughtfully carried a basket of strawberries up. A new climb followed by strawberries at the foot of it—what more could one wish for!'

My first experience of climbing Tophet Wall was at the end of an active day with Ed Cleasby when we soloed the route. Of the routes we had climbed that day, all considerably harder, it is Tophet Wall that lingers most in the memory; proof enough of its special qualities.

The Wall itself is situated in an impressive position high on the traditional climbing flanks of Great Gable. It overlooks a mighty shoot known as Great Hell Gate and the exposure is felt even before the climbing begins. In all about 200 feet (61m) high the Wall to the left and directly above the line of the route overhangs considerably. The rocks are strikingly angular, almost as though they have been clean cut with some supernatural blade, and the Wall is monolithic with no tousle of greenery to break the spell of verticality.

There is no easier route on the Wall and the line is therefore the most logical climbing solution to this impressive piece of rock. At few stages in its entire length is it possible to break off or deviate onto easier ground and the climbing remains remarkably sustained and technically interesting. It has, then, the essence of a memorable climb.

The first crack, gained from the right, is immediately steep and keeps you moving until better holds on a small ledge can be grasped and a steep pull made to a rest. A grooved ramp cutting the lower wall, is followed until grass ledges and flake belays deposit one beneath a solid vertical barrier. The original route traversed to this point from the right, across easier ground, and it took Kelly some while before he could solve the problem of this steep obstacle.

It is still quite a bold proposition today and the angle hasn't relented any. But effort is rewarded with a series of small but positive holds leading up to a horizontal break, enabling the huge corner groove on the left to be gained. This follows, again technically, until one can belay beneath the imprisoning overhangs of the top headwall.

Escape is made by the spectacular rightward traverse, naturally formed, between the overhang above and overhangs below. Anything this lacks in difficulty is more than compensated for by the extent of exposure. Yet, fittingly, it is the last pitch which is both the more difficult and the most airy, a splendid finale to a sparkling route.

Lately I revisited the route with Tony Greenbank (author and survival expert) and his son, Mark. It was an abysmally wet day,

Mark and Tony Greenbank in the grooves on first pitch, Tophet Wall.

moved tentatively across the exposed, slimy traverse. Some way across he stopped. Because of the audio difficulties all communications were being relayed through myself on the ground. Unable to see through thick cloud, or hear his father, Mark shouted down to me, 'Can I climb?'

'No,' I replied. But Mark had set off.

'Get back,' I shouted. The clouds swirled and lifted to reveal Tony, his feet no longer dazzling red and black but brilliant white. Fitting of any survival expert worth his salt he had removed his boots and proceeded to climb in stocking feet. I shouted my approval and Mark shouted up again, 'Can I climb yet?'

'Who are you trying to kid?' I thought, and responded:

'You're not bad son,' but he was on his way again.

Theirs was a good effort in adverse conditions and all were elated on their safe arrival back to the foot of the climb. Tophet Wall is a route attractive enough to be enjoyed in any conditions, though personally, I think an ascent during the strawberry season is to be preferred.

Above left: **Mark Greenbank approaching the bottom crack.**
Above right: **On the steep wall, second pitch.**

brightened only by an abundance of good humour, yet I felt optimistic, for after all, what could befall us with such an assemblage of talent? At Seathwaite Farm we stopped and chatted to Stan Edmondson (winner of the Senior Guides Race at Grasmere Sports on three occasions) for we were in no particular hurry to rise into the 'clag' and rain-hugging the tops.

When we could delay no longer we set off. At the wooden bridge prior to Styhead Tarn, Tony showed us a sizeable boulder, now toppled over, that used to be a test-piece in nailed boots. We examined it and asked Tony if they managed it with no hands. 'No way,' he exclaimed and apparently hurt continued at an uptempo pace fitting, one would imagine, of a nailed Tiger of the past.

On arrival Tophet Wall was found to be dripping wet, with intermittent rain and dense cloud making it a formidable challenge. Nevertheless

nothing ventured, nothing gained . . . and the Greenbanks set-to with a vengeance—I remained on the ground! It was one of those occasions, due to the eerie atmospherics, when the leader could not hear the second and vice versa.

High on the traverse, after some impressive leading in dire conditions by Mark, Tony

THE LAKE DISTRICT: Slip Knot

SLIP KNOT: 150ft (46m). Severe (Hard).
First Ascent: R.J. Birkett, L. Muscroft, 25 May 1947.
Location: White Ghyll, Great Langdale, Lake District.
Map Ref: 298071.
Guidebooks: *Rock Climbing in the Lake District* by Birkett, Cram, Eilbeck and Roper. *Great Langdale* (F&RCC Guide) by M.G. Mortimer.
Attitude: Faces west.
Altitude: 100ft (305m).
Rock: Rhyolite.
Access: Start from the New Dungeon Ghyll Hotel/Stickle Barn (large car park at the side or smaller car park at the edge of the road opposite Hotel entrance) where White Ghyll can be seen as a nick in the skyline up to the right. Follow the path to cross a little bridge over a stream just above the Hotel. Continue along this path through a gate to gain a wide, open track—after 100yds (30m) a stile leads rightwards to a narrow path which is followed along the wall and under the wood to gain the bottom of the Ghyll itself. Straight up the Ghyll to a lone tree (sycamore) situated beneath the first set of crags (Lower White Ghyll). Immediately above lies the attractive cracked wall of Slip Knot (25 minutes).
Descent: From the top of the climb traverse leftwards (looking *in*) and go *up* a rake (*not* down the scree as this drops over the cliff) over rock steps—to descend back into the bed of the Ghyll (Upper White Ghyll towers above).

Slip Knot – Summary

Above the tree there is a right-angled corner, topped by a large block overhang, with a clean and attractive wall to its right. The climb takes this wall then traverses left under the overhang to gain the steep rib. Start at the base of the corner a few feet up from the bed of the Ghyll.

1. 70ft (21m). Up the corner until a right traverse, across flake holds, gains the crack in the middle of the wall. Straight up this to belay on the rock ledge to the side of the overhang.

2. 80ft (24m). Traverse left, beneath the overhang, until a long stride enables the exposed rib to be gained. Climb directly up the steep rib until a heather ledge is reached. Belay well back.

Slip Knot – Description

My first impression of White Ghyll was made when, as a youngster, standing in my brother's (then) farmyard at Side Farm I chanced to look up to see the lower rocks of the gorge bathed in the evening sunshine. There, in red, a climber was making his way up

SLIP KNOT

belay point

climber

Above: **SLIP KNOT: 150ft (46m).
Severe (Hard).**
Far right, top: **Tony Greenbank
looking down the wall.**
Far right, bottom: **John Lockley on
the cracked wall.**

done some climbing'. Sure we'd walked and scrambled on the fells and hills ever since I could remember, and sometimes ropes had been involved, but it hadn't been rock climbing and, quite honestly, I found it hard to believe! An intriguing situation to have started rock climbing not knowing that your father had been a leading protagonist, but such was the case.

For the rock climber, even years on, the power of White Ghyll does not diminish. Very few of the hordes of walkers inhabiting Langdale, pass through the Ghyll, and most who assemble here mean business. The whole place basks in a hallowed atmosphere, with the all-prevailing influence being that of bare rock; rock strewn all around you at your feet, the bed of the Ghyll, and rock soaring and bulging above—climber's rock.

There are two sections to White Ghyll—the upper and lower crag. The upper is the most formidable looking and consists of a continuous wave of overhangs ending with the sharply contrasting, pleasant, buttress of the Slabs 1 and 2. Once tree-covered and extensively vegetated, the lower buttress is now clean and attractive. Perhaps the lines here are not so blatantly spectacular as on the Upper Crag, but they are striking and their execution proves to be exciting enough.

White Ghyll was first introduced to hard times with Jim Haggas's ascent of The Gordian Knot (VS) a remarkably daring venture taking the centre of the overhanging mass of the Upper Crag. Subsequently Jim Birkett took over development, producing a host of fine climbs on both upper and, after a mysterious wide-ranging fire that layed the rock bare, lower White Ghyll crags. Of these, he always thought Do Not to be his best and most neckiest lead (contrary to guidebook information, a direct bottom pitch was made) but as far as quality goes there are a number of routes concentrated here which are worthy of mention.

On the Upper Crag, Haste Not (VS) and White Ghyll Wall (MVS) contrast markedly but offer uncompromised exposure and on the lower crag Slip Knot (HS) gives an absorbing climb with, again, distinctly exposed situations. Modern development has yet to improve the situation and there is now a super large collection of excellent routes in the Extreme category. Despite all these worthy contenders my choice of route, based purely on a personal level, was easy.

Slip Knot was one of the first routes I climbed in the Ghyll and I found it, as they say in the vernacular, a real trouser-filler! Because of this, and the committing undercut and

the clean face of Do Not. To me it looked stupendously impressive, even from that distance. It's hard to fully describe the intense feeling of excitement, but it was an emotion so strong that I instantly knew that I had to be a rock climber. Nothing less would do.

So, I made a start with a mate from school only to learn in mum's words, 'Your dad's overhang position gained on the second pitch, it is a difficult route to grade subjectively. Originally it was given Severe, subsequently this rose to Very Severe, but I think a realistic compromise rests at Hard Severe. Starting the route is no problem as big holds take you rapidly up the corner of the wall. It is only when moves right are made (best to place a runner high in the corner, to step back down before moving right) that the sense of position is felt—as the bed of the Ghyll drops rapidly away below you. But holds are generally good, delightfully hard rock with square-cut flakes, on which balancy moves are followed by large positive footholds and a rest before a straight crack is tackled. Steep but straightforward, this leads to a sizeable rock ledge and nut belays in a crack at the end of the distinct black overhang. Care should be taken to get a good belay as the next section is not overly endowed with runners.

The ledge, a horizontal oasis in a desert of vertical and overhanging rock, enables one to relax and enjoy the scenery before tackling the next, radically different, section of the route. Immediately above lies the steep challenge of Do Not, where I spied that climber in red many years ago, and below, the wall just climbed which, when viewed from above, looks alarmingly steep. Looking outwards to the right of this, there is a smooth-looking right-angled corner forming an undercut rib. The wedge-like rib, which tapers from nothing out of the depths below, is the precarious-looking objective of the next 20ft (6m) of the climb, only to make matters a little more impressive, the corner and wall are capped by a very large menacing black overhang.

It is, however, the easiest line to follow from the ledge and is therefore the most deserving way through the rock desert. Part of the problem with getting your mind to realise this and consequently your body to perform the necessary actions, is the fact you're leaving a haven of security to face all-too-obvious exposure and difficulty. Initially you get bunched up, on large flat holds, and have to force yourself to uncoil, court the steepness below and commit yourself for the security of the corner. Once there, sometimes a little damp seeps unsympathetically down and over the best hold, and it is quite a tricky business reaching the rib. It is not far, but far enough to force you to extend yourself into at least a couple of moves, ultimately involving a long stride to the edge.

Once you actually pull onto the rib you feel 'out there' but elated; happy that you made the commitment; a tremendous sense of satisfaction as the surge of adrenalin gently subsides.

Above left: **John White on the first pitch**.
Above right: **Tony Greenbank on second pitch, 'going for the slap'**.

Delicate footwork up the rib leads to bulging rocks culminating in a little overlap, but you'll scarcely notice these. From there on it's plain sailing to a large heather terrace.

Taken along with any of the other routes I've mentioned or as the only route on a short day, in the morning shade of a hot summer's day, or alternatively in an evening when the sun warms the rocks, it's a colourful climb requiring just a little bit of a push. It is because of this latter quality, I feel, that its ascent is an experience that will be remembered when others have faded into obscurity. A good introduction, also, to harder things.

When I first set out on the climb, I wouldn't have dared class myself as a rock climber. Afterwards, with my first Severe lead successfully accomplished, I felt I was. One other thing I eventually plucked up courage to do was ask 'him' directly if he started the fire that made it all possible. He looked me coldly in the eye, categorically denying it with a single word and that's as close as we ever got to talking about Slip Knot.

THE LAKE DISTRICT: Eve

EVE: 165ft (50m). Very Severe (–, 4b, 4a).
First Ascent: W. Peascod, B. Blake, 11 August 1951.
Location: Shepherds Crag, Borrowdale, Lake District.
Map Ref: 264185.
Guidebooks: *Rock Climbing in the Lake District* by Birkett, Cram, Eilbeck, Roper, *Borrowdale* (FRCC Guide) by D. Armstrong and R. Kenyon.

Attitude: Faces west.
Altitude: 300ft (91m) (low lying, dries quickly).
Rock: Borrowdale volcanics.
Access: On Borrowdale road from Keswick (3 miles, 4km), sited on left between Lodore and Borrowdale Hotels. The crag lies immediately above the road and parking is either in a small space directly below or on side of the road near Borrowdale Hotel. Eve lies on the middle most

Above left: **The view up to the groove on second pitch.**
Above right: **The crux.**

117

EVE

O belay point

1st pitch
obscured
by trees

**EVE: 165ft (50m). Very Severe
(-, 4b, 4a).**

(north) Buttress. This is the highest, most striking, buttress and is marked by a fallen tree
across the path near to its toe and by a deep
groove up the wall to its left (Ardus). Approach
directly or traverse along underneath crags
(Brown Crag on left, Chamonix area on the
right) (5 minutes).

Descent: Down a gully leading to scree shoot
on the right.

Eve – Summary

Start left of the toe of the buttress above a
splintered block (approximately 50ft, 15m,
right of the deep corner groove of Ardus).

1. 45ft (14m). Up the slab rightwards until a
crack leads to a ledge and spike belays.
(Harder is to gain the ledge by hand jamming a
steep crack to the right, near the toe of the
buttress—4b. This is the first pitch of Adam.)

2. 70ft (21m), (4b). Up the groove until a
long stride can be made leftwards to the edge.
Go up on to the slab and continue diagonally
leftwards (balancy with poor protection), then
straight up to a small rock stance and good nut
belays (high up). This is on the edge of the
large open corner groove (Ardus).

3. 50ft (15m), (4a). Up to the overhang then
steeply follow the diagonal crack breaking
rightwards. Continue along this then up to the
top of the crag.

Eve – Description

Often scorned by the big mountain men,
Shepherds Crag nestles, seductively, in the
trees just above the narrow Borrowdale road;
offering a wide range of short, quick drying
rocks. The afternoon and evening sunshine,
even in mid-winter, radiates from her rocks
and a good climb can be had here, all year
round, often when other Lakeland crags are
positively dripping and repulsive. There are
many fine climbs of all grades of difficulty and
although short and popular there are some
that have an exclusive charm about them. The
provocatively tempting groove and slab of Eve
is just such a route; offering bold and balancy
climbing, a delight of movement and of
exquisite technique.

Eve first fell to Bill Peascod and Brian Blake
on a summer's evening in 1951. Outwardly it
was merely a chance affair, they had been
elsewhere during the day and turned up on
Shepherds to 'knock off' some of the establishment routes before darkness. As one would
naturally expect, Bill's roving eye spotted the
delectable line immediately above the path; a
little slab leading to a well-defined groove, in
turn giving access to the beckoning slabby wall
stretching an attractive 80ft (24m) or so to the
top of the crag.

It became the final of his quartet of routes,
all named in honour of notorious women, and
all climbed in 1951: Cleopatra, Delilah and Eve
(with Brian Blake) and Jezebel (with Stan
Dirkin). The names were reserved for routes
with special qualities and with the naming of
Eve there was an extra bonus—a free pint in

the nearby Scafell Hotel! The barmaid's name was, purely coincidentally, Eve.

My first acquaintance with the lady was made long before I met Bill Peascod or had even heard of his name. I was bored during the school holidays, so hitched through to Shepherds intent on doing some climbing.

From Ambleside right to the Lodore Hotel I got a lift in a Rolls Royce! There was only one snag—the driver and his wife were religious fanatics intent on converting me to their particular beliefs. I couldn't relate to it. Outside the sun was beating down through a clear blue sky, the canopy of leaves above the road diffusing the light into an intermittent cool green. Derwentwater shone blue and silver and the rocks reflected a beckoning purple brown. All I wanted to do was climb, I ached for it. Outside was my simple reality. To touch the rocks, smell sweet clean air and bathe in the crystal-clear waters of Borrowdale was my idea of holy action. They seemed blind, reeling forth their inflexible ideals whilst passing through, and ignoring, some of the most beautiful country on God's earth. I felt that the price I paid for the ride was high and on completion of my day's activities I walked back to Langdale in the gathering darkness, worshipping every single, lonely, minute.

On arrival at the crag I was wound tight, like a spring, and frantically leapt at the rock until tired arms gave sufficient excuse to seek out Grange Bridge and plunge into its cooling depths. I must have soloed around a half-a-dozen routes from Diff. up to Very Severe and was particularly satisfied with Slings (HS), which I found the hardest of them all and Fisher's Folly (VS), a climb particularly suiting my, then, preference for wide bridging. But of all the routes climbed on that particular day, Eve gave me the most pleasure.

Soloing is not an art I would even pretend to aspire to in any significant way. Nevertheless, it does have certain undeniable qualities: the obvious ones of rapid movement, freedom and flexibility and some which are not so easily explained. It is difficult to generalise because these qualities are an extension of the individual's personality, but for me these include the feeling of being alone, of putting my life on the edge and of baring my soul. Somehow it gives one a clarity, a chance to look at oneself clearly, possibly to find yourself, but factually and unpretentiously. I only do it either if I feel I'm going to enjoy it or if I haven't got anyone else with whom to climb. Both instances being a very rare occurrence.

Eve is the kind of route you may as well solo, even with today's protection, but it's not that fact which makes you do it. It beguiles you with a simple slab and crack leading from tree-shaded gentle rocks to a sunlit, naked, rock groove. But beware, once tempted, a swing left made from the top of the groove on to delicate slabs makes it very difficult to turn back. After only a little way the good holds become significantly smaller and the slab rears into a wall. Here delicate moves upwards are made with no meaningful protection whatsoever. It has been the scene, unfortunately, of a number of fatal slips.

Confidence, coolness and ability are the requirements necessary for success. Bill Peascod described his feelings on the first ascent to be those of someone 'indulging in a death-defying act', but when he reclimbed the route, leading it in his sixties, he found it easy. In his book *Journey After Dawn* he wrote:

'As it was, I enjoyed it, and was relaxed on every move. My attitude of mind had been conditioned by the security I felt in my footwear and safety gear.'

This attitude of mind is, of course, the climber's most important asset.

After the crux is passed the climb continues pleasantly, but still steeply, over an overlap to a stance on the rib overlooking Ardus, another highly recommended route. The rock above now overhangs, but a crack, with both good holds and plentiful nut runners, provides the key to reaching the upper section of the wall. Pleasant climbing and easy scrambling leads to a host of tree belays and the calming vista of Derwentwater stretched out not far below.

Whilst 'mountain men' may disdain the crag, if they spend any time at all in the Lake District they will ultimately, one wet day, find their way to Shepherds. They may even be tempted by the intriguing and delightful little Eve, fatefully to taste the fruit of knowledge. Shame on them, but then again, why not, or as Bill would say 'Why not mate, it's bloody there!'

Bill Peascod's first ascent description in Birkness cottage.

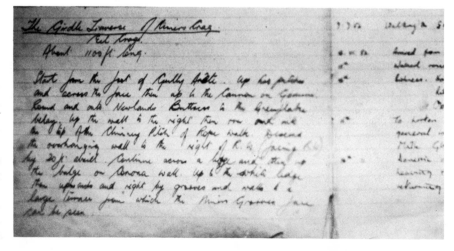

THE LAKE DISTRICT: North-West Arete and 'F' Route (Combination)

Gimmer Crag with a fine view to the Langdale Valley below.

NORTH WEST ARETE: 135ft (41m), (4b). Mild Very Severe.
First Ascent: R.J. Birkett, V. Veevers, 1940.
'F' ROUTE: 160ft (49m), (4c). Very Severe.
First Ascent: R.J. Birkett, V. Veevers, 1941.
Location: North-west face of Gimmer Crag, Great Langdale, Lake District.
Map Ref: 277069.
Guidebooks: *Rock Climbing in the Lake District* by Cram, Eilbeck, Roper. *Great Langdale*

(F&RCC Guide) by M.G. Mortimer.
Attitude: Faces north-west.
Altitude: 1,600ft (488m). Dries quickly.
Rock: Rhyolite.
Access: From either the New or Old Dungeon Ghyll Hotels.
New: Take path leftwards to cross the Dungeon Ghyll and follow steeply rising, zig-zagging path until plateau. Continue along until branch left leads to South-East face of Gimmer (small path

off the main Pikes track).

Old: Take steep path trudging up scree on left to eventually reach a well-defined narrow path which leads to the South-East Face of the crag. The former is the most obvious route to follow. (Both about one hour's walk.) On reaching the face drop down to the toe of the vegetated rocks and climb steeply back up the other side until the North-West Gully is reached (15 minutes).

Descent: Into North-West Gully via Junipall Gully—an awkward, steep descent, or to South-East Face via South-East Gully—easier but still steep! Gimmer Crag forms a head separated from the hillside by these two obvious gullies which both start at the same point, but South-East Gully can be entered from a lower point so dispensing with a few feet of scrambling above the climbs. Finding this point is not easy, the gully walls are elsewhere vertical, so if in doubt continue up and back to the source of the gullies.

North-West Arete – Summary

Where the track enters the gully is a steep wall on the right. The climb starts on the left side of this initial wall, from the bed of the gully, and moves up to follow the distinct arete.

1. 135ft (41m), (4b). Up the Wall and move right to a groove leading up through the overhang. Up this groove, crux, to a good flake from where a rightward traverse leads to the exposed arete, Climb the arete directly to gain the large Ash Tree Ledge (no tree). Continue up.

'F' Route – Summary

From the same belay on Ash Tree Ledge.

1. 160ft (49m), (4c). Easy rocks lead up towards the magnificent corner (the feature of the route). Continue up to a small ledge then

Above left: **Tony Greenbank on the wild corner of F Route.**
Above right: **Tony Greenbank and Frank Davies on the North-West Arete.**

121

N.W. ARETE AND F ROUTE

F Route
obscured

possible belay

bottom section
obscured

O belay point

NORTH-WEST ARETE: 135ft (41m), (4b). Mild Very Severe.

The north-west aspect of Gimmer Crag is one of the finest in the Lakes. This is the rock climber's crag where the ground is steep and clean. At its highest it plunges precipitously for almost 200 vertical feet (61m) into North-West Gully—giving some of England's most classic rock climbs. In fact the whole of Gimmer could be considered to be as aesthetic a piece of rock as can be found anywhere. It stands poised on the steep sweeping fellside between the famous Langdale pikes (Harrison Stickle and Pike of Stickle) like a great circular citadel on the brink of a precipice.

To select a single route to do this particular piece of rock justice is exceedingly difficult: there are so many eminently fine ones to choose from. Ultimately I decided on the logical combination of North-West Arete and 'F' Route, two routes in name, both tackling obvious features, both offering high quality climbing of Very Severe standard. Linked, they give a direct and flowing line up the crag.

NW Arete doesn't, despite its airy position overlooking the NW Gully, blazon itself upon you. The climbing seems to side-step quietly up the wall, though with a surprisingly rapid increase in exposure, until suddenly confronted with a barrier of overhangs. Here with harder, steeper rock to the right, it takes the bull by the horns and follows a steep groove channelling through the bulge. This looks, and is, quite hard but protection is good and the holds, when they arrive, are great sinking flakes.

At the top of the groove you can rest and place excellent protection and then, with the crux behind you, savour the tip-toeing moves out to the edge of the arete itself. Initially belays were taken up on the edge, but with modern double rope techniques and correct use of equipment, extending runners allowing one rope for the wall and one for the arete etc., allow you to just head on straight up.

Climbing the arete is pure joy; basking in the exposure and pulling and balancing on small but positive holds. There is something very elegant about climbing an arete, it feels right as though it is positively the exact place to be—I suppose simply you know when you're on line. This one is also enhanced by the fact that it is perched in the air, being considerably undercut at its base.

Once you're up, on to the substantial Ash Tree Ledge, the next challenge is glaringly obvious. 'F' Route is the penetratingly steep right-angled corner hanging about 100ft (30m) above your head. Overhanging slightly, it is the

move up to the overlap on the left and through it using a good flake above. Continue to the overhang (at the bottom of the corner—possible tiny stance). Step right and climb the steep corner crack. Crux at the top. A few feet more leads to belays and ledges on the right.

most feasible line up this fiercely impressive rock. The last of the alphabet routes to be climbed, it is a wholly fitting conclusion. All start from Ash Tree Ledge and work their way round from SE to NW ascending in difficulty; how appropriate the hardest and 'bloodiest' should be named 'F' route!

A bit of a scramble up easy rocks leads to a narrow ledge and the start of the climbing proper. (It's possible to move belays, but if your ropes are long enough, Ash Tree Ledge is comfortable, the belay is good and the view enthralling, so why bother?) It immediately feels steep and imposing and the adrenalin begins to surge in anticipation of the crux still a long, long way above. Fortuitously, the climbing is hard enough to make you concentrate and forget all but the immediate rock and the essential task at hand.

I think it was Dougal Haston who pointed out that the only time you fall off is when you lose concentration and let your mind wander away from the actual climbing moves you're making. There's a fair degree of truth in this philosophy, enough anyway to succour and comfort the determined but gripped climber. Dad (Jim Birkett) simply told me to always stay cool and calm, 'Just relax. If you're going to fall off there's nothing you can do about it by getting uptight.' Coming from someone who never fell off in the whole of his climbing career it has to be sound advice. But the crunch comes when putting these theories into practice.

Still, keep on going and soon things begin to unfold nicely. Good holds above the overlap lead you to move up the wall above and bang your head on the overhang, the bottom overlap of the overhanging left wall of the corner, before you know it. Traditionally, a stance was taken here offering, perhaps, a false sense of security before the imposing corner. Today it is best to pass this by as it's a mere one-legged perch with heartily indifferent belays.

Then you're there, in the corner, the object of the route, and all you have to do is climb it to the crux, situated where it should be, right at the top. Layback, bridge, jam—an exhilarating climb, the epitome of the Very Severe grade.

Afterwards, to descend back into North-West Gully it is necessary to scramble up until the head of Gimmer Crag stands proud from the rest of the hillside. Junipall Gully plunges back down at this point and this should be followed with a degree of caution. It is most often slimy and there are a few awkward rock steps to negotiate before a rib, on the crag side

of the gully, can be followed more easily downwards.

Stone axe 'roughings' can be found readily in this vicinity, a legacy of the industries of pre-history. The strong-willed, and environmentally conscious, will not remove them, but merely take their photographs, leaving them for future generations to appreciate and enjoy. But the climber will most probably hurry on down to the fine 'amphitheatre' just above the start of NW Arete and from the open rib on the outside of the gully sit eating sandwiches admiring the sun-soaked rocks and famous rock climbs towering above.

It is difficult to imagine a greater collection of so many distinguished routes in such a small area. Each with its own particular characteristics, each an honoured representative of its grade. From left to right: Gimmer Crack (MVS) the 1920s challenge; Gimmer String (E1) of the 1960s; Kipling Groove (HVS), the hard route of the 1940s and *the* route to climb for the aspiring 'hard man' for decades after, Equus (E2) an elegant line of the 1970s; Midnight Movie (E4) a hard and direct line of the 1980s, and finally North-West Arete and 'F' Route would all be my selection of routes not to be missed.

After Gimmer Crack the next most obvious line, the corner on the other end of the bulging upper face, was 'F' Route. Jim Birkett looked over the top to assess its possibilities, but at that time thought it unclimbable. It is easy to understand why, for looking down this impending stretch of rock does make an envisaged ascent look distinctly desperate. Remember there were no nut runners, or any likely forms of protection on that top crack, in those days. A year later 'Just because we were on Ash Tree Ledge' he decided to give it a go. 'It isn't hard at all, is it. There are good holds all the way. Hell it must be simple today with all that stuff you carry around.'

Even so, I think he was wearing rubbers, but he had been laced into his trusty 'Nails' ('waisted clinkers' for the discerning) the previous year for his ascent of North-West Arete. This apparently was a pretty casual affair, with Jim stopping for some considerable time en route to chat with fellow climbers in the amphitheatre below.

Interestingly on the same day J.W. Haggas and Miss E. Bull were opening up the central section of another major Langdale crag with their ascent of the bold and difficult Gordian Knott in White Ghyll. In time others would follow!

OVERHANGING BASTION: 235ft (72m).
Very Severe (4b, 4a, 4c+, –).
First Ascent: R. J. Birkett, C.R. Wilson, L. Muscroft, 1 April 1939.
Location: North Buttress of Castle Rock, Thirlmere, Lake District.
Map Ref: 322 197.
Guidebooks: *Rock Climbing in the Lake District* by Birkett, Cram, Eilbeck and Roper. *Buttermere and Eastern Crags* (FRCC Guide) by Ed Grindley and G. Higginson.
Attitude: Faces west.
Altitude: 1000ft (305m).
Rock: Volcanic (Volcano Plug) running to flake holds.
Access: Plainly visible from the main Ambleside-Keswick road (A591) it is approached from the constructed car park on the St. John's-in-the-Vale road (B5322). Walk across to the empty-looking farm building and go through the gate. (Alternatively go straight across the road to a stile.) Follow the track, taking the left-hand route when it joins another. Go up to cross an aqueduct and gain the wood just below the crag (15 minutes).
Descent: Either down a steep gully to the left (moderate scrambling) or a circuitous journey round to the right over then beneath the south crag.

Overhanging Bastion – Summary

From the large buttey stone, walk right for 30 yards (27m) to where easy climbing leads to a comfortable multi-tree ledge at 35ft (11m). A corner groove on the left is the first objective.

1. 65ft (20m), (4b). From the left end of the ledge go up the wall to gain the groove. Continue up ramp/groove to ledge and flake belays.

2. 40ft (12m), (4a). Continue up slab to where it steepens, this is the base of the pinnacle, move blindly left to find a good ledge and an 'any nut' crack belay.

3. 65ft (20m), (4c+). Gain the top of the pinnacle and precariously move onto and up the gangway. Move left at the top, on good but hollow flakes, and up to reach the gnarled old yew.

4. 55ft (17m). Continue up gangway or climb out right and then up to top.

Overhanging Bastion – Description

Travelling from Ambleside to Keswick as you speed past the end of Thirlmere Lake (hidden over to your left), you can't fail to spot the great bastion of rock on your right. Legend says that a magical and mysterious fortress, the Castle of St. John, guards the slopes below the mighty Helvellyn, however when the traveller attempts to reach the castle it disappears to reveal nothing but a 'terrible pile of stone', its two main towers, contrasting, but both giving the impression of verticality and impregnability. The south tower is the lesser and its warm bubbly rock has a friendly disposition. The north tower is grander, one of Lakeland's finest faces of rock, and leans gently over from the ground to its turrets 250ft (76m) above.

Guarding the entrance to St. John's-in-the-Vale it is now known as the castle rock of Triermain, famed by Sir Walter Scott's poem 'The Bridal of Triermain' and to climbers by Jim Birkett's ascent of the 'Overhanging Bastion'.

'No Misty phantom of the air,
No meteor-blazon'd show was there;
In morning splendour, full and fair,
The massive fortress shone.'

Up the middle of the buttress lies a bold and striking ramp—this is the line of Overhanging Bastion. At the time the ascent was headlined 'Lakeland Everest Conquered'; I suppose its nearness to the road, and the fact it is in full view of every Lakeland tourist, resulted in this extensive and dramatic media coverage. But then again it was a tremendous lead for 1939 and, psychologically at least, a major breakthrough in standard.

Despite its size and impressiveness, Castle Rock is an attractive and friendly crag. In the afternoons (stay on the south crag in the mornings), it becomes a sheltered suntrap and, if the crag isn't actually weeping after a prolonged period of rain, it dries quickly. The very best time to go to Castle is in the spring sunshine, when an April sun warms the rock and nature is awakening after the harshness of winter. This is the time, also, when the rock climber can emerge after the winter fast, stretch the muscles and experience those crag senses of smell, touch and movement—all stirred by the promise of summer.

All Fools' Day, April 1st, was the day the lads made their ascent. They wore rubbers. Jim recalled the day wasn't brilliant, but they had a couple of hemp line slings to see them on their way 'Easy for Very Severe, the hard move right next to the belay—but reasonably exposed'. He means it too, because that's how he found it. But for me and you the truth is, it is quite hard for Very Severe, with the main pitch, stepping off the pinnacle and gaining the ramp, still committing, balancy, technical and bold.

At sixteen with a pair of F.E.B. mountain boots, a mate from Manchester who couldn't care less about reputations, and a few Severes and a Mild VS on East Raven all to my credit, I led OB. I couldn't say my ascent was a cruise

Far left: **Castle Rock**.
Below: **Steve Hubbard moving on to the ramp-crux**.

OVERHANGING BASTION ROCK

Yew belay

The Ramp

crux stepping on to ramp

wet corner

scramble to ledge

belay point

Above: **OVERHANGING BASTION**: 235ft (72m). Very Severe (4b, 4a, 4c+, -).

Above right: **Dave Lyle in the initial groove.**

Far right: **CLEOPATRA**: 230ft (70m). Hard Very Severe (4c, 5a, 4c).

but then I didn't find it all that bad either.

The first real pitch starts from the tree ledge (just right is another J.B. classic—May Day Cracks VS—and left another—Zigzag VS) and is gained after a scramble up a nice little juggy wall. It is short wall to gain a corner groove and at the time it was oozing slime and greenness. This proved to be awkward, but soon dried out above to give enjoyable climbing to a large flake belay. Here the ramp starts to find form and steepens until moves

left round the pillar, low down, give access to a spacious ledge, good belays, and high exposure.

The next pitch is the great one and now free from the shroud of trees the moves to the top of the pinnacle, below the hanging ramp, are airy in the extreme. From its top a precarious step gives access to the ramp. Commitment is required, the crux to be climbed, before good holds and adequate nut protection is reached.

From below you imagine the ramp to be almost the ultimate in exposure. Well it is, but it's bigger than you imagined. It wraps you up like a favourite armchair, comfortable and secure. Things change at the top. You must traverse left, quitting security, on rickety flakes and here there is no compromise with position. You know where you are, with clear space to the ground 200ft (61m) below.

Belayed on the gnarled old yew you know it was a doddle really, a classic, magnificently straightforward. Now you can relax and know the fulfilment of a good climb. And perhaps, if you have time, spare a thought for a young lad, his hemp rope, his eye for a line, his two rock-steady partners, and that ascent almost fifty years ago.

Or as Sir Walter Scott said in his poem 'The Bridal of Triermain':

Dare no more!
'That would I' said the Warrior bold,
'If that my frame were bent and old,
And my thin blood dropp'd slow and cold,
   As icicle in thaw;
But while my heart can feel it dance,
Blithe as the sparkling wine of France,
And this good arm wields sword or lance,
I mock these words of awe!'

CLEOPATRA: 230ft (70m). Hard Very Severe (4c, 5a, 4c).
First Ascent: W. Peascod, S. B. Beck, 1951.
Location: Buckstone How (Yew Crags), Honister Pass, Buttermere, Lake District.
Map Ref: 223143.
Guidebooks: *Rock Climbing in the Lake District* by Birkett, Cram, Eilbeck, Roper. *Buttermere and Eastern Crags* (F & RCC Guide) by I. Roper.
Attitude: Faces south-west.
Altitude: 1200ft (366m).
Rock: Slate (generally sound but caution should be exercised).
Access: From the Honister Pass, dividing Buttermere from Borrowdale, take the old Quarry track directly above the Youth Hostel. This ends in a slate scree which should be crossed, low, to gain the right-hand end of the crag (10 minutes).
Descent: Traverse right to descend a rake which is the top edge of the crag. *Great care must be taken to avoid knocking loose slate onto anyone below.*

Cleopatra – Summary

Goes up the first continuous large wall some 100ft (30m) left of a distinct clean-cut groove. A grass rake slopes up left, below some overhangs. Start right of this from a rather shattered little pillar. Scramble to the top of this.

1. 80ft (24m), (4c). Step off the pillar and through the overlap rightwards to gain a leftward-sloping gangway. Follow this to a crack and up this until an exposed traverse, on pockets, rightwards can be made across the steep wall. Gain a rock ledge stance. Poor belay.

2. 65ft (20m), (5a). Step left and up the tricky rib until a traverse left can be made into the left most of two grooves. Up this to step left to a belay left of the overhang.

3. 85ft (26m), (4c). Move back right and make an awkward move through the overhang to gain a groove. Up the groove and trend left to a ledge below a futher groove. Go steeply up this and left edge to the top of the wall.

Cleopatra – Description

Often described as *the* roadside classic of the Lake District, Cleopatra combines accessibility with quality. From your car, conveniently parked at the summit of Honister Pass, a fifteen-minute pleasant stroll finally tumbles you across a scree fan of quarry debris to the foot of the climb. First impressions are

CLEOPATRA

descent

climber at
the stance

crux

climber

◯ belay point

Above: **Buckstone Howe amongst the slate workings.**
Right: **Paul Cornforth and Tony Sibley crossing the wall on finger pockets.**

deceptive; the crag and the climb appear to be short and rather broken, but in truth the climbing becomes a sustained piece of work with each move absorbingly interesting.

Honister Pass may not be the steepest or biggest in the Lake District, but its wild and domineering surroundings certainly register it as the most impressive. Fleetwith Pike muscles hard against the little road which plunges steeply into the head of Buttermere Valley with Honister Crags rearing above black and massive. Slate holds the greatest interest in the whole wild, inhospitable composition. Its influence is inescapable, both in the rocks and in man's workings for it. Below the crags the scree runs fall and fan to tickle the very sides of the Pass and above, huge black caverns, ramps, roadways, bridges and red-rusted steel hawsers wind intricately and alarmingly into a heart of stone.

Outwardly it is a strange setting for a Lakeland crag, and it is a climb of distinction, for one expects natural beauty, not as we have here, an obvious mix of man's influence (quarrying) and the innocent green charm of Buttermere. Nevertheless, it is a wonderful composition of great depth, brought to life when the sun turns the stream silver and highlights the incomparable grey-blue greens of the slate. Honister crags are always black but Buckstone How (Yew Crag) and Cleopatra are favoured by the afternoon sun—this is the time to climb here.

The crag and the climb dry exceedingly quickly in summer and can be found suitable for climbing within minutes of it ceasing to rain. Because of this, despite its height above sea level, it often proves to be a worth-while venue for early or late in the season, when many Lakeland crags are too wet or cold. Situated amongst plunging slate screes the crag occupies an airy perch with views right across Honister and down to Buttermere Lake, giving remarkably interesting climbing reaching its best on Cleopatra.

Although the rock is slaty, as long as one recognises this fact, it is reasonably sound and, on Cleopatra, although the rock often feels smooth, almost frictionless, the nut protection is quite reasonable. Predominantly the crag is structured of ribs and walls with an abundance of grooves often replacing the walls. The route, complex to describe, is totally logical in execution and follows a technically absorbing sequence of moves, virtually without respite, for a distance of some 200ft (61m).

The first overlap, stepping from a rather shattered pillar, leads onto the immediately vertical, and apparently blank, wall. A ramp and a groove give no clue until suddenly a line of tiny pockets lead rightwards across the vertical wall. These are the key and they take you across the blue-green, white lichen-splodged rock in a series of moves that belie the steepness of the situation.

Soon a large ledge is reached, I don't remember the belay as being particularly outstanding, and with the benefit of modern gear, two light ropes and a good variety of smallish nuts, some parties lead out the second and first pitches as one. Whatever you choose to do, the difficulties remain the same and the rib is, again, balancy, hard and fairly serious—the crux of a technical climb. Following this it continues to unfold with all the panache and excitement of a good novel. Up front it always looks improbable, as though the next series of moves will commit you to unclimbable ground, but after each move that vital hold always appears. Each move, too, requires thought—it's not a climb just to be muscled up.

Moves left lead you into a little groove high on the wall and above there juts a large, perfectly flat-bottomed, overhang. You move up, tentatively and with trepidation, towards it, but, thankfully, before you reach it a swing left gives access to a small rock ledge and belay.

Now you go over it (and it's good value), to gain the aesthetic straight-lined symmetry of the groove above. Below there is a lot of space: your second and the rocks beneath have vanished, tucked in underneath the overhang. A magnificent route with a very modern flavour: imagine it, if you can, with only a few line runners for comfort!

A good climb is defined by so many different qualities and each individual has his or her own ideas on just what is good. Personally I regard Cleopatra as one of Bill Peascod's best rock climbs—he thought so too. No doubt you will form yor own opinion and that is how it should be. But be there as the evening draws in and the day surrenders to a cool, smoky dusk so you can watch the sun setting over Buttermere. We were, Bill and I; that's the time to be on Buckstone How.

Paul Cornforth on the crux rib, second pitch.

THE LAKE DISTRICT: Central Buttress

Above: **Scafell Crag.**
Far right: **Bill Peascod astride the great flake.**

CENTRAL BUTTRESS: 470ft (143m). Hard Very Severe (4b, 4b, 5b, 4c, 4b).
First Ascent: S. W. Herford, G. S. Sansom, C. F. Holland (H. B. Gibson and D. G. Murray on first ascent of Flake), April 1914.
Location: Scafell Crag, above Wasdale, Lake District.
Map Ref: 208068.
Guidebooks: *Scafell, Dow and Eskdale* (F & RCC Guide) by G. Willison and M. Berzins. *Rock Climbing in The Lake District* by Birkett, Cram, Eilbeck, Roper.
Attitude: Faces north.
Altitude: 2,500ft (762m).
Rock: Rhyolite.
Access: From Wasdale take the track starting by the stream near the car park at the head of the lake. The way is obvious and rises very steeply via Brown Tongue to gain first a horizontal stretch (Hollow Stones) and then a large boul-

der at the rim of the cwm below the crag. Churn up the steep scree shoot on the right to gain the horizontal traverse of Rake's Progress. Start left of the large gully (Moss Ghyll) in the centre of the crag by scrambling up to a broken ramp (1 1/2 hours).

The approach from Borrowdale is long and arduous. From Styhead follow the Corridor Route across the top of Piers Ghyll and so into Hollow Stones (2 1/2 hours).
Descent: A path leads down towards Mickledore (in direction of Scafell Pike) and ends in a series of polished steps (Broad Stand; Moderate) or down Deep Ghyll to the west, descending along a path down its Westerly flank, to gain the steep bottom section of Lord's Rake (obvious chimney rift).

Central Buttress – Summary
The original route is described without any

variations. Start after scrambling beneath a rock ramp in the centre of the crag about 50ft (15m) left of the obvious gully splitting the crag (Moss Ghyll).

1. 50ft (15m), (4b). Up the ramp.

2. 80ft (24m), (4b). Go up and left to a crack and climb this to gain the left end of a large ledge (The Oval). Go horizontally right to beneath the great flake crack.

3. 65ft (20m), (5b). Up the crack to the chockstone and pass this until bold moves enable the knife-edge top of the flake to be grasped. Traverse left along this to belay awkwardly but safely.

4. 30ft (9m), (4a). Continue up and along, passing a jammed pinnacle to descend to a square ledge.

5. 50ft (15m), (3b). Go along the ledge and up the ramp to block belays.

6. 75ft (23m), (4c). Move down and then traverse delicately and boldly right, passing a rickety pinnacle to a corner. Up this and move again delicately rightwards then up to step right to a v-rock ledge. Poor belays.

7. 60ft (18m), (4a). Move across the ledge to gain the wall on the right, around the corner. Make an ascending traverse across this to gain a sizeable groove/slab (Moss Ghyll Grooves). Up this to a large boulder-strewn ledge.

8. 60ft (18m), (3c). Up the wall left of the gully and then easier rocks on the left are climbed to a short balancy wall. Up this and continue directly to the top.

Central Buttress – Description

Because 'CB' is so famous, cliched, and popular, I for many years avoided it like the plague. When people said 'You mean you haven't done CB?' I would smile and inform them that this was one I was saving for my old age. I meant it.

A rather remarkable man, Bill Peascod, changed this situation for me—with his infectious enthusiasm for life in general and climbing in particular, Bill thought CB to be the single most distinguished Lakeland route he had climbed and described it in his book *Journey After Dawn* as having a unique blend of size, steepness, character, quality of climbing, difficulty and atmosphere that made it incomparable. This was recommendation enough and on one rather damp and greasy day we set off to climb it.

Scafell is a mighty lump of rock, the pride and focal point of Lakeland rock climbing, and the rock for climbing stretches in a long semi-circle from the Shamrock up to Deep Ghyll Buttress and then, growing in stature, arcing round through the Pinnacle, Pisgah

Buttress, Scafell Crag and finally on the Eskdale side of Mickledore, the East Buttress. All steep and impressive ground and all, on the Wasdale side of Mickledore, dominated by the highest and steepest face of rock; the daunting Scafell Crag. Here a 250-ft (76m) vertical wall intimidates both eye and mind seemingly exhibiting no weakness, no compromise, in its domination. Yet, on interested inspection, beneath a faint wisp of a horizontal crack, a magnificent leaning groove, only initially hidden by the sheer size of the wall, plucks at the heart of the climber. This is the Great Flake and provides the key to a great climb—Central Buttress.

The boys were playing on the rocks around Moss Ghyll when they spotted the Great Flake:

'The rock fell away very steeply below and a sheer smooth wall rose up to a great height above; its regularity was interrupted at one point, it is true, by an enormous rock flake which tapered out to nothing 70 feet higher. . . The Great Flake looked quite hopeless as a means of ascent and we dismissed the idea at once.'

wrote G. S. Sansom in his article 'Scafell Central Buttress'.

The following year they returned but were turned back at the flake, and shortly after this Sansom went to Brazil for the summer. Herford's letter which reached him there spelt out the inevitable:

'We then made an exploration of the CB. We found that it will go without serious difficulty except the top 20ft of the flake crack.'

They finally put it in the bag in 1914. Even allowing for the fact that Herford stood on Sansom's shoulders, whilst Sansom had lashed himself to the jammed chockstone near the top of the flake crack (in fact I'm far from convinced that this would make it easier) and that they worked on the route, it was a very bold and brilliant effort. It still is!

C. F. Holland wrote, in his *Climbs on the Scafell Group* (FRCC Guide, 1926):

'*The Central Buttress:* The most arduous ascent in the Lake District; unexemplified exposure; combined tactics and rope engineering essential at one point; not less than three climbers. Rubbers.

'The ascent of this buttress, the final problem presented by the great facade of Scafell, was made for the first time in April, 1914. It has as yet been repeated on two occasions only, and the difficulties met with are so great that the expedition ranks among the world's hardest, and is possible only under practically perfect conditions.'

All was quiet at Hollow Stones as Bill and I approached, and the clouds rolled menacingly up and down the crags. The atmosphere was dark and forbidding, the rocks were damp and greasy and it was the kind of day when one fully expected to see Herford's ghost walk unobtrusively past. A huge wet streak ran down the wall from beneath the chockstone of the Great Flake and I realised that the climb for my old age was in fact going to be a sizeable and difficult undertaking.

I set off, feet slipping and sliding, and found the so-called easier pitches up to the Oval absolutely desperate. Secretly I hoped Bill would want out and present me with some

CENTRAL BUTTRESS: 470ft (143m). Hard Very Severe (4b, 4b, 5b, 4c, 4b).

CENTRAL BUTTRESS

Moss Ghyll

boulder-strewn ledge

rickety pinnacle

v. ledge

Great Flake

The Oval

ramp

Central Buttress

Rakes Progress

Moss Ghyll

belay point

reasoned case for so doing. But I didn't, then, fully appreciate the tenacity or depth of character of the man.

He climbed those wet, greasy slabs with grace and style, proving he was still the master of precarious balance climbing. There was not the faintest hint of wanting out. Then it was up to me and I knew we were going up, greasy rock, or no.

The Great Flake from the Oval is very steep and, not so obvious from the ground, rather overhanging. It feels as though it's going to be demanding even before you start, and, as proved by the multitude of falls and failures seen at this point, it is. Under the prevailing conditions it was going to be an entertaining proposition.

Fortunately the wet streak stopped at the chock and the crux above looked dry. So up to the chock I went, all the time feeling worried and insecure. The protection is little better than 1914. Pretty soon I was clipping the cluster of old tat round the chock and, with a faint heart, wrapping my own long sling round it, too.

I attempted it at least three times, with skidding feet and pumping arms, each time retreating to the poor rest below the chock. Conflicting advice ran through my troubled mind:

'Jim (Birkett) jammed it, in nails. In nails! Dolphin laybacked it.' Gazing down to the Oval and Bill, patiently belaying, was an alarming feeling, I got the impression of being on a big crag, in a way out positon and the grade of HVS at that time seemed entirely meaningless. I've climbed countless routes that have been graded much harder and yet rarely experienced such a powerfully gripping fear.

Shouting down to Bill I got the first word in. 'It's all in the mind, I'm going to layback it next go, so watch the ropes.'

Bill chuckled on the ledge. 'Dolphin fell off lay-backing—in nails'. But I'd got a grip and was definitely going to go for it.

'Watch us' and I went. Once I had made that mental commitment it wasn't so bad and it actually felt like there was a good hold after a few scary moves.

I shouted down—'There's a hidden jug', as you do, and proceeded to grab the top, a wafer-thin edge, the ultimate handhold.

I was interested, now, to see just how Bill, then 62 years of age and re-ascending the route after some 38 years, was going to cope. After various contretemps with my threaded sling and clipped in-situ gear, necessitating him to go up and down three times, he still powered up the edge like a cork exploding from a champagne bottle. An exceptional per-formance.

The mist lifted, the sun shone through and we laughed and hollered, as only climbers can. Bill, subsequently wrote in his autobiography, *Journey After Dawn'*:

'It was the kind of moment that will live in a climber's memory as long as life.' It's a sentiment, that I'm sure, Herford and Sansom felt, a feeling of trying and winning and the joy of sharing something unique.'

The climb by no means ends at this point and the traverse across the upper wall, high above the Great Flake, gives delicate climbing with breath-taking exposure. We took the original finish, a traverse across into the final groove of Moss Ghyll Grooves, as this seemed a fitting and logical end to a satisfying route. For my part, if someone ever asked me to recall one of my finest days out on the mountains, I would tell of the day I climbed the immortal Central Buttress with young Bill Peascod.

Bill Peascod nearing the V ledge with mist swirling about him.

THE LAKE DISTRICT: Footless Crow and Tumbleweed Connection

FOOTLESS CROW: 180ft (55m), E5 (6b).
First Ascent: P. Livesey, 1974.
TUMBLEWEED CONNECTION: 190ft (58m), E2 (5c, 5b).
First Ascent: P. Botterill, D. Rawcliffe, 1976.
Location: Goat Crag, Borrowdale, Lake District.
Map Ref: 265165.
Guidebooks: *Rock Climbing in the Lake District* by Birkett, Cram, Eilbeck, Roper. *Borrowdale* (F & RCC Guide) by S. Clark.
Attitude: Faces north-east.
Rock: Borrowdale Volcanics.
Access: Drive up the Borrowdale valley from Keswick and turn right over a narrow bridge to enter the tiny hamlet of Grange. A narrow road leads off to the left and ends at a camp site. On the right a stile leads to a track up the fellside and to the crag (visible from the camp site). It is probably best to follow the track along by the wall after crossing a stream and then zagging right to follow the rake under the crag. The climbs lie on the right side—up the largest buttress on the crag (15 minutes).
Descent: Abseil from trees either directly down Footless Crow (50m ropes *just* reach) or over to the right (looking in).

Footless Crow – Summary

On the right side of the crag is the Great Buttress. Start in the centre of the Buttress by scrambling up 25ft (8m) to a shallow groove about 15ft (5m) right of the district corner groove (Praying Mantis).

1. 180ft (55m), (6b). Up the groove to where it bulges. Pull into the niche and straight up to gain a rightward sloping ramp. Continue along and up to reach a cluster of bolts (possible stance here) below the overhangs. Up to the left there is a flake with a bashed-over peg, above this gain an undercut then a further undercut (Friend 2½ placement on its left-hand side). Move down left from this (low left foothold) to make a long reach to a vital layaway hold beneath an overlap (crux). Step left again until a crack provides an excellent hold and good protection (Friend 1½). Step left again, then up the green wall to reach overhangs (no further protection to top). Pull leftwards through these and up the slabby wall. Move left to cleaner rock on the left and finish up a shallow groove and wall to heather ledges

Paul Cornforth running it out to the bolts.

and tree belay high up. (The original route continued straight up, but this is distinctly vegetated and dirty.)

Tumbleweed Connection – Summary

Start immediately left of the distinct corner groove (Praying Mantis).

1. 90ft (27m), (5c). Follow the hand traverse left to the edge then pull straight over into a shallow scoop. Move up (tree runner high on right) then across and down left using a crack (runners), move up to a small roof, then left to the obvious weakness leading straight up the wall to piton runner. Go right, stepping low, to gain a groove on the edge and climb it to tree belay (junction with Praying Mantis).

2. 100ft (30m), (5b). Follow the break leftwards until above the traverse a shallow groove leads up the wall. Follow this and the continuation of the groove leading to the overhang. Move leftwards through the over-hang to the arete and climb the slab above.

Footless Crow and Tumbleweed Connection – Description

Footless Crow climbs pretty much directly the great overhanging main buttress, free climbing the old aid route 'Great Buttress'. Tumbleweed Connection takes an attractive and intricate line up the blank-looking lesser buttress to the left. Both routes offer good steep clean rock, very much in the modern idiom, and give difficult but immensely enjoyable climbing. Two classic and popular 'extremes' little more than ten minutes from the car—what more could the modern rock athlete ask for?

The line taken by Footless is breathtakingly spectacular and climbs through a sea of yellow overhangs all leaning menacingly over a daunting grey vertical wall. It is big and fearsome with a free ascent looking naive in the

Below left: **Pinching the first undercut**.
Below right: **The crux**.

FOOTLESS CROW: 180ft (55m), E5 (6b).
TUMBLEWEED CONNECTION: 190ft (58m), E2 (5c, 5b).

extreme. Livesey's ascent in 1974 shattered the established rock climbing scene and its rapid reassemblement, with renewed vision and greater horizons, was the foundation for the next decade of British rock climbing development. Pete Livesey had realised the potential of athletic training and this coupled with the application of modern techniques (utilising small wire nut, in situ protection and abseil inspection and cleaning prior to an ascent) and a reckless audacity to try, with the absolute determination to succeed, gave climbing an immense leap forward in technical standards.

The name Footless Crow was given to the route because being so overhanging and with no place to rest, the climber must keep moving—hopping from one minute hold to the next never daring to stop. It's an imaginative name for an innovative climb. A name every discerning 'Extreme' leader has on his 'hit' list.

I believe when I first tackled it there had only been a handful of successful ascents, anyhow it was the first attempt of that season. The bottom section involves climbing a corner groove until a bulge is met, and steep, strenuous moves are necessary to first gain a recess and then the bottom of a natural gangway leading diagonally up rightwards across the great grey wall. Intimidated, moves into the recess were thwarted by an abundance of moss and lichen, and I came back down. But who should be at the bottom to witness the retreat? Only Pete Livesey. He enjoyed it, maybe not so much as the first ascent, but he certainly enjoyed it. I felt sick!

A few days later I was back. Another team (Rob Uttley and Pat MacVae) had attempted it in the meantime but they, too, had been beaten by the moss on that first section. This time I was with a very enthusiastic second, Colin Downer, and this was all the fillip I needed. An additional spur was the presence of a number of climbing heavyweights scattered across the crag. Dave Armstrong and the Carlisle lads over to the left, Bernard Newman and girlfriend on Praying Mantis, Martin Berzins and Chris Sowden on Mirage Direct. The pressure was on and failure, in such exalted company, quite out of the question.

The first section up the ramp had been made considerably cleaner by the previous attempts and went straightforwardly at around 5c/6a. The ramp itself gives superb climbing, technical, but always with plenty of positive holds and before you know it you're on the stance bristling with old bolts and a peg. I met Martin on the stance (shared with Mirage Direct) and received a few words of cold comfort before I stepped up and left to attempt the formidable overhanging barrier.

Knowing how to do 'Footless' makes it considerably easier, for the moves through the overhangs are, by necessity, cunning. From a rickety flake with bashed-up peg and rotting wires you make moves up steep ground on two large undercuts. The second, larger, undercut

FOOTLESS CROW AND TUMBLEWEED CONNECTION

top slab obscured

top undercut

crux

bolt belay

peg

crux traverse

Footless Crow

scramble

Tumbleweed Connection

belay point

gives a Friend 2¹/₂ placement, making the moves relatively safe, before a move out and down leftwards, to a tiny foothold, enables a 'rock-up' to reach a side pull beneath an overlap (6b).

A quick pull through and a vertical crack can be stuffed with gear before green-stained rocks lead steadily but spectacularly to the next roof. The climbing is now quite easy, though from the roof to the top (about 50ft (15m)), there are no worthwhile runners. I followed the original line up unstable vegetation and rock, and this was easily the most dangerous section of the climb, but it is better and wiser to move leftward into a shallow groove (Praying Mantis).

Despite taking a number of falls from the crux (just testing the gear of course) I found myself the first, of all the teams climbing, to the top of the crag—it was a good feeling. Colin had been climbing as I had been making the final moves, our 165-ft (50-m) ropes not being long enough to complete the route. But it didn't present a problem; on arrival he was as elated as I was.

Down below the thinly ginger-haired Geordie figure of Dave McDonald hopped and wailed. We threw down the ends of the ropes which he somehow managed to reach and up he came. 'Why man, Footless, it's incredible.' We were all in hearty agreement.

In some respects Tumbleweed Connection, although a considerably easier proposition, is the greater pioneering effort of the two climbs. I mean this in the sense that Pete Botterill was the first to find and climb his line, whereas Livesey on Footless, as on many of his climbs, climbed an existing aided climb free. On Footless the ground had been covered before, on Tumbleweed the rock was virginal.

Tumbleweed is a beautiful piece of climbing, a line giving both delicate and bold movement so typical of Peter Botterill's many great contributions on Lakeland rock. It opens with an immediately exposed traverse leftwards, from Praying Mantis, a gentle introduction, but soon a precarious balance move up, leading to a little scoop, gives a taste of what is to follow. Round the corner, on the left, hovers the main face of the buttress, the challenge of the route, and this is gained on rapidly steepening rock. Left of an overlap the vertical wall is climbed directly and confidence is the key here, for the runners rapidly sink way below. It is exciting climbing until a piton is clipped and one can pause and take in the situation with a more relaxed air. A technical toe-tapping, leg-stretching, traverse right (crux) leads to the edge and big insecurity until the substantial tree belay of Praying Mantis is reached.

The next pitch is of equal quality, and possibly more imposing, with the difficult moves so obviously capped by a sizeable bulk of impending rock. The final groove is followed with trepidation until, wonderfully, one can pull leftwards through the overhang, in an incredible position, to gain the final easy-angled headwall.

Below stretches the beautiful Borrowdale valley, Derwent Water and over in the distance the oft oriental-looking Skiddaw smiles down inscrutably. It can't fail to be a good day whichever route you choose. Two very different routes, perhaps, but both big in their own small way.

Paul Cornforth gaining the scoop on Tumbleweed.

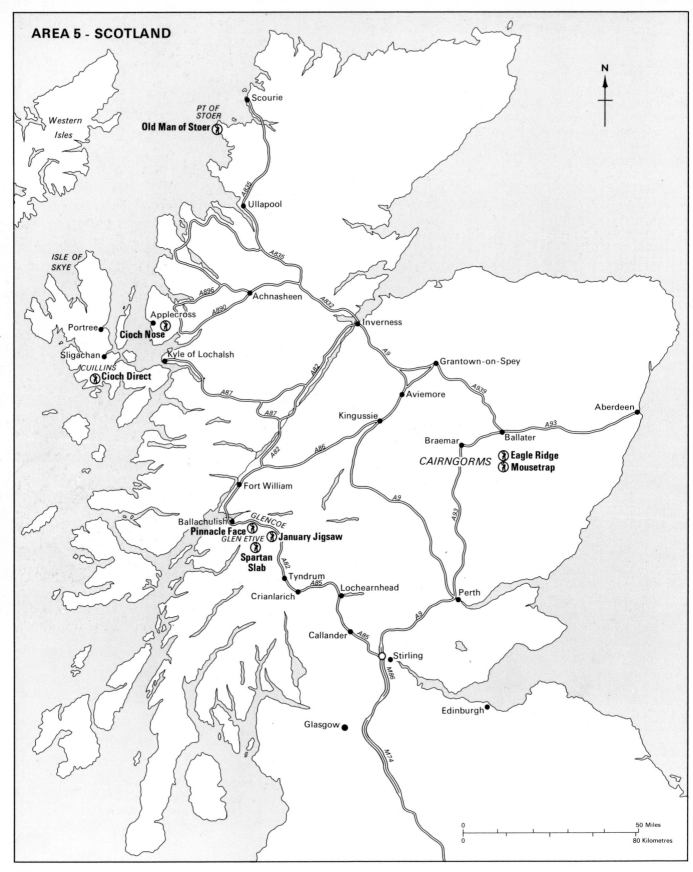

AREA 5 - SCOTLAND

Western Isles

PT OF STOER
Old Man of Stoer

Scourie

Ullapool

ISLE OF SKYE

Portree

Applecross
Cioch Nose

Sligachan

CUILLINS
Cioch Direct

Kyle of Lochalsh

Achnasheen

Inverness

Grantown-on-Spey

Aviemore

Kingussie

Braemar

CAIRNGORMS Eagle Ridge
Mousetrap

Ballater

Aberdeen

Fort William

Ballachulish
Pinnacle Face

GLENCOE

GLEN ETIVE January Jigsaw

Spartan Slab

Tyndrum

Crianlarich

Lochearnhead

Perth

Callander

Stirling

Edinburgh

Glasgow

0   50 Miles
0   80 Kilometres

138

SCOTLAND, The Pinnacle Face

The Pinnacle Face: 300ft (91m). Very Difficult.

First Ascent: J.H.B. Bell, C.M. Allen, May 1932.

Location: B. Buttress, West Face of Aonach Dubh, Glencoe, north-west Scotland.

Map Ref: NN 144 556.

Guidebooks: *Scottish Climbs 1* by Hamish MacInnes. *Glencoe and Glen Etive* by Ken Crocket.

Attitude: Faces north west.

Altitude: 2000ft (610m).

Rock: Sharp-edged rhyolite. Splintered flakes require care.

Access: Start where the A82 forms a junction with a narrow road leading to the Clachaig Inn. Climb over the SW corner of the bridge and follow the path up towards Coire nan Beith. Take off left, crossing the stream, below the lowest water-fall and follow the path up a sharp

The west face of Aonach Dubh. A broad gully lies to the left, B. Buttress is immediately right of this.

Inset: **John Hargreaves on the pinnacle.**

THE PINNACLE FACE

O belay point

**THE PINNACLE FACE: 300ft
(91m). Very Difficult.**

eroded edge. Directly above is the Dinner-Time
Buttress (Descent Path). Cross back over to the
right and continue up B. Buttress (first right
then scrambling back left) via the vague path.
This leads directly to Middle Ledge (the obvious
horizontal break that traverses the entire West
Face of Aonach Dugh) and The Pinnacle Face.
(1¼ hours).

Note that although No. 2 Gully lies immediately left of here there is no summer access
from Middle Ledge to No. 2 Gulley (and so out
onto Dinner Time Buttress).

Descent: From the top of the Pinnacle Face go
over leftwards to follow The Rake dropping
down into the top of No. 2 Gulley.

Follow down No. 2 gulley for a short way
only until one can move out onto Dinner Time
Buttress. To the right looking out. (There is *no*
safe descent down No. 2 Gully.) Descend down
Dinner Time Buttress with a moderate rock step
nearing the bottom.

The Pinnacle Face – Summary

Start up a chimney about 30ft (9m) left of
where the approach path hits the Middle
Ledge (this is right of a large vegetated
groove).

1. 100ft (30m). Climb the chimney, moving
along left, after the first vertical section, along
an alarming (but apparently safe) detached·

block to pull up a further short vertical section
and out right onto the face. Move across right
a few feet to poorish spike belays.

2. 45ft (14m). Continue up the grassy slabs
and corner left of the shattered arete to a ledge
below a further black corner chimney.

3. 60ft (18m). Climb the chimney, awkward
to enter, to a cave below the capstone and pull
out over this with difficulty. Continue over to
the right to belay in the corner.

4. 45ft (14m). Up the corner, care with loose
blocks, to stand beside a large pinnacle. Move
up to take a belay on a flake and small ledge
below a crack running up the right side of the
great pinnacle.

5. 50ft (15m). Up the crack, transferring left
into the steeper corner crack and then right
again onto the wall. Continue more easily up
to the top of the pinnacle.

Move up the ledge and between the gap can
be seen the renowned Pinnacle Flake. It is
customary to scramble into the gap (protected
with a rope from above) and up onto the
Pinnacle for the photograph.

From here moderate, but exposed, scrambling, to the right, leads to the main buttress
(don't go high immediately as you're on a
pinnacle). Continue rightwards and up to the
top of the buttress.

The Pinnacle Face – Description

The West Face of Aonach Dubh is the most viewed and readily apparent feature in Glencoe. From the Clachaig Inn and the free camping either side of the road, lit by the evening light, it is a most appealing sight. Because of its relative accessibility and uncomplicated nature it serves as an extremely worthwhile introduction to climbing in the Coe. It is also a route, as I think the photographs illustrate, that can be done in wet conditions—a strong feature for any Scottish route.

Accepting the above, it is also a day out even worthy of those who know the Glen, for it is a pleasant mountain situation, amongst super surroundings, with moves exercised on hard rhyolite. It is also a varied climb with thrutching and awkward chimneys, face climbing and a steep crack near the top. Overall the position is stimulating and, because of the quite large detached and splintery rock flakes that occur periodically, sound mountaineering judgement is essential.

Still in my sleeping bag I reclined gracefully along the rear of John Hargreave's van. On one side perched a pint mug of hot coffee, on the other a greasy plate and the bony remnants of brown trout, which I had caught in a nearby burn the previous day, in my hand a humorous book (Alastair Borthwick's *Always a Little Further*). I thought nothing could be more satisfying than being warm, comfortable, well fed, with a good read, whilst listening to the rain pinging on the metallic van roof. With quiet confidence I had written the day off to sublime laziness.

The double van doors flew open and a maelstrom of cold, wet air rushed in.

'Right matey, let's go to it!' Why, oh why, are people so keen? I sulked at the injustice of it.

But it's different once you have made the transition. Once you have committed yourself to being cold and wet and have thrusted yourself forward to another epic—it actually feels as though you're enjoying it. I suppose it's that little extra effort that makes us climbers, rather than just philosophers or anglers!

'More boring rainbows,' joked John as we headed up for the West Face of Aonach Dubh. Multitudinous rainbows again flitted up the Glencoe Valley—doubles, singles, huge arcs, weak grins—the poor summer of 1985 if for nothing else, should be remembered as the 'Year of the Rainbow'.

Most of my climbing hereabouts had been on the harder classic routes—Big Top (HVS), Trapese (E1), Hee Haw (HVS)—or soloing the gullies in winter, so I was looking forward to exploring another area of the face. On reaching the Middle Ledge and locating the start of the Pinnacle Face I took a reccé left to determine the connection into No. 2 Gully. Despite indications in most guides to the contrary, in summer, it's just not there. A vertical vegetated wall of 'horrendous horror' separates the two. So take note and be warned and think twice about leaving your gear at the foot of the climb.

The initial chimney is quite awkward, then it curves over, still remaining a wide chimney, and becomes technically easier. But this section, especially in the wet, is a lot scarier as it feels precarious and one must move over, pulling and eventually stepping on, a sizeable block that appears completely detached.

Mixed climbing with a little vegetation thrown in for interest takes you to the definite crux. A fairly short chimney in a corner—short, but full of interest. A classic exercise in jamming, bridging and, if you tackle it in any way like myself, wild 'hope there's a better hold up here somewhere' thrutching.

After this the position becomes interesting. It conveys the impression that you are on a big mountain face. The huge pinnacle up above has to be climbed as escape would be hazardous due to the possibility of dislodged loose rock doing serious mischief and behind you now two smaller pinnacles seem to enhance this feeling of commitment.

Delightfully, the top wall, although steep, goes at a reasonable grade and leads to a resoundingly large ledge. My feeling on reaching this point, with person and camera gear all soaking wet, was of immense elation. But where's the Pinnacle Flake? For a minute both John and I felt cheated. Then we spotted it and with howls of insane laughter completed our pilgrimage.

Climbing is many things to many different people. Sometimes for me it is the pure hard technicality that is the most important. This is my bias. But sometimes it is the joy of simply being in the mountains. On other occasions it's the company that means the most. Today, despite the weather, had been a great day on the hills.

As John wound his van up to a sizzling 50 mph, and I dozed off, as usual, to the roar of the engine, I recalled the words of the 'Cragsman' by Geoffrey Winthrop Young:

'For all of beauty that this life can give
   lives only while I live;
And with the light my hurried vision lends
   all beauty ends.'

The crux chimney on the third pitch.

SCOTLAND: The Cioch Nose

Above left: **Luke Steer on the difficult corner groove of the second pitch.**
Above right: **The airy stance before the third pitch.**

Far right: **On the upper section looking down to the Cioch itself.**

THE CIOCH NOSE: approximately 640ft (195m) of Very Difficult climbing and much scrambling.
First Ascent: C. Bonington, T.W. Patey, 1960
Location: The Cioch, Sgurr a Chaorachain, Applecross (near Kishorn), North-West Scotland.
Map Ref: NG 797427.
Guidebooks: *Scottish Climbs 1 & 2* by Hamish MacInnes.
Attitude: Faces east.
Altitude: 1300ft (396m).
Rock: Torridon sandstone, sound and rough.
Access: Take the Applecross road off from the A896 Lochcarron to Shieldaig. Either approach

from Russel Bridge, parking by bridge, from where the Cioch Nose can be seen from the car, via an indefinite track on west of Lock Coire nan Arror (1¼ hours) or descend from the VHF Aerial mast near the summit of Bealach na Ba. The latter is distinctly easier (approximately 40 minutes) and has the advantage that the route is continued over various peaks and gaps to naturally finish at the aerial. For the latter, take the car to the summit of the pass and then continue to mast. Follow a ramp down (westwards) beneath cliffs and skirt round the bottom of Sgurr a Chaorachain, along the valley until the Cioch Nose is reached.

Cioch Nose – Summary

Scramble up the lower buttress to the shelf below the overhangs of the Nose. Start, just about on arrival at the shelf, up a groove left of a noticeable large belay flake (left of the Nose itself).

1. 130ft (40m). Up the corner groove and climb directly until the last corner leads awkwardly to a substantial ledge and belays (peg in situ).

2. 50ft (15m). Move right to obvious chimney groove and climb this awkwardly. At the top step right to an airy, large block, belay on the edge of the Nose.

3. 80ft (24m). Step right then go straight up the wall for about 25ft (8m) (peg runner on right) until moves lead leftwards to easier ground. Continue straight up to stance (keeping left of an overlap).

4. 100ft (30m). Move right to pick the easiest groove to a further belay ledge.

The climbing now becomes substantially easier and leads in about 200ft (68m) (best climbed together or solo) to the top of the first hump (Cioch).

Continue over this across the gap and scramble up the upper buttress until the ground again steepens and a further pitch of rock climbing (80ft 24m), right of the gulley, leads to the top of the second hump.

Continue along the ridge over peaks and hollows towards the VHF mast.

Cioch Nose – Description

As is always the case with Scottish crags the walk to the Cioch, from the Russel Burn Bridge, looks like a five-minute affair. In practice, not running, it takes over the hour. I suppose I should have known, having experienced this deception on countless occasions, but it was the 'Och man, no longer than a few minutes—it's next to the road' advice from a friendly Scot that threw me. It's not that I dislike walking (in truth I rather enjoy it) just that it's rather disconcerting to misjudge these things.

Indeed walking, the approach and descent from the climb, and being amongst the mountains is an integral part of Scottish climbing. Walking gives you time to appreciate the precious mountain environment and should be valued rather then bemoaned. The Cioch Nose epitomises the total mountain adventure of Highland climbing and that is not to say the line itself isn't bold, challenging and exposed. On first acquaintance, in fact, one could be forgiven for assuming that this towering bastion of rock would not yield to a climb of less than Extreme standard.

The climb takes you not merely over spectacular and challenging rock but also up the front face of two large buttresses leading directly onto the summit ridge. Combined with the approach either from Russel Bridge or the VHF mast there is something more to such a day than the thrill of rock climbing alone, for the experience is filled with many different elements, the intrinsic joy of rock climbing, the appreciation of nature, the satisfaction of route-finding, the appeal of conquering a peak

and if you're particularly lucky, as I was, the sharing of your day with an equally appreciative and affable companion.

Considering the facts surrounding the first ascent I feel almost embarrassed even mentioning the paltry walk from Russel Bridge. For in 1960 Chris Bonington and Tom Patey spent a day, naturally enough Patey being Patey, of epic proportions. Disembarking from the train at Stromeferry, they crossed to Strome Cas and, unable to obtain a lift, walked the 12 miles (19km) to Sgurr a Chaorachain. Arriving at six in the evening they embarked on the route in a heavy downpour. On its successful completion they continued a further 5 miles (8km) to arrive at the Achintraid Youth Hostel shortly before 11pm.

Chris and Tom were at that time two young servicemen (I think 25 and 28 years old respectively) with boundless energy for climbing. Chris described this holiday in 1960 where he and Tom climbed ten new routes, often solo, in almost as many days: 'It was a fantastic summer, we had a whole series of epics, hitching and busing from climb to climb. After the Cioch Nose we climbed King Cobra (then naming it Alligator Crawl) on Skye. Every day was a magical mystery tour with my great friend Tom Patey. A fabulous guy.'

We too, Luke Steer and myself, arrived at the crag in the rain with the ever-threatening rolling clouds finally closing over the climb. Luckily the approach had been clear, giving us ample views of the spectacular Cioch. The Cioch itself is usefully split into two distinct levels. The lower 300ft (100m) or so is, apparently, rather broken and disjointed, but the upper section consists of an impressive corrugation of grooves and ribs curving round the Cioch, each seeming at some stage to end in an overlap. Resultingly there appears to be an endless series of lines to be climbed, but with the proviso that, because of the overhangs, they will all be extremely hard.

It is a matter of surprise then that the climb itself is of a reasonable standard, indeed the first ascensionists were prepared for an extreme route. Even so there are some interesting moves and the climbing situations, after the first pitch is over, are tremendously spectacular and exposed. Even from directly below, the crucial pitch looks well in excess of its actual grade.

A fairly well worn trod leads up the steep grass and broken rocks to gain the left-hand end of the horizontal shelf. Above this and along as far as it goes you could climb virtually anywhere if you were prepared to climb hard enough. Patience is required to pick out the most sensible (and often used) line. We settled

THE CIOCH NOSE: approx 640ft (195m). **Very Difficult.**

CIOCH NOSE

best scrambled

scramble approach

○ belay point

for a short groove, left of the distinct over-hangs, which lead via walls to a corner, which in turn lead to the commodious belay ledge. Here pegs mark the spot and relieve the feeling of exploration, serving no other useful purpose as there are countless natural and nut belays to be had. This start was just left of a sizeable flake belay which, in addition to the fact that it was the most obvious feature reached on arrival at the shelf, seemed incentive enough to climb it.

When you see the deep chimney groove on the right you know you are on your way and the next stance confirms the route's reputation for exposure. Luke looked like some pensive eaglet huddled on the tiny rock ledge. Discerning enough to shelter from the soddening rain but ever eager to take flight. It was a perfect location to do so, as you are now on the very edge of the Cioch with nothing but beckoning space all around. Below is hundreds of feet of nothing until, through the mists, can be seen the lush green of the grass, the purple and grey rocks and the rich black peat bogs of the typically Scottish Highland valley sweeping down grandly first to Loch Coire nan Arror and then on to the sea (unfortunately one can also, all too obviously, see man's corruption in the form of a multi-million pound oil platform construction site on the shores of Loch Kishorn). The situation instils a powerful feeling which only the privileged few, an eagle or a climber, can fully experience.

From this position of immense exposure the beetling wall above looks very hard; difficult to the point where one is tempted to climb elsewhere; however, elsewhere appears even less feasible. So up you go expecting the worst.

For our part, Luke placed a nut directly below the wall and I moved the belay over to get a better view. As the rain died and the clouds rolled a little higher, he set off climbing rapidly, proclaiming it steep, even technical, in places but all in all, deceptively straight-forward.

Initially, he climbed directly then moved rightwards to clip an in-situ piton which was unnecessarily placed by a previous party as the climbing is by no means precarious and a nut placement would serve equally well. But we clipped into it anyway—I suppose a classic case of 'Curse it then clip it'. Steepening ground now suggested to Luke that he went left and this indeed proved the key to keeping the climbing standard within its reasonable grade. Soon he was heading up again and with the occasional enthusiastic comment, only identifiable as enthusiastic by the pitch of the sound as the clarity had mingled undecipherably with the wind and rain, he was soon up to

the next ledge stance, out of sight, some 80ft (25m) above.

An inspiring pitch, (Bonington called out to Patey 'Come on man—it's incredible'). It brings the route to life as a technical climb. Much of its delight and quality is owed to the properties on the rock. Torridonian sandstone is extremely hard, greater than six hundred million years old, and runs to a variety of good handholds. Although not obvious from below, it abounds with pockets, neat ledges and spikes, all giving holds of superlative quality. Additionally its rough structure (often in the form of bands of quartz pebbles strongly cemented together with a finer sand matrix akin to, but tougher than, gritstone) gives tremendous friction. Because of this it has infinite climbing possibilities—even when wet, an exceedingly important factor for any Scottish rock climb!

Afterwards I moved right to seek the easiest corner groove from the variety of possibilities above. Then really only scrambling remained for a couple of hundred feet to the top of the Cioch. It is probably best to climb Alpine style here, taking loops of rope.

Continuing across to and up the upper buttress one can look down on the narrowing head of the Cioch and again enjoy the exposure, observing the vertical curtain of purple-grey rock sweeping endlessly down into the depths. But the climbing is still not over. A final pitch at the top of the buttress with some unnervingly large tottering pinnacles, is climbed, on the left, with some interest. This section successfully negotatied, it is wise to continue right along to the end of the ridge, aiming for the VHF mast, as a number of the gullies leading prematurely down contain considerable rock steps which bar a safe descent.

We took a rather damp walk back down to Russel Bridge, satisfied with our climb, taking time to catch and photograph a few of the multitudinous frogs which leapt every which way across our path. For Patey, his ascent was the realisation of an eight-year dream—the dream of a man who knew and loved the remote and beautiful coast of Scotland like no other, before or since. There could be no finer recommendation for a route than this.

The incredible third pitch.

SCOTLAND: January Jigsaw

Above: **Buachaille Etive Mor.**
Far right: **John Hargreaves out to the edge on second pitch.**

JANUARY JIGSAW: 250ft (76m). Very Difficult (Hard).
First Ascent: H.I. Ogilvy, Miss E. Speakman, January 1940.
Location: The Rannoch Wall, (South-East Face) of Buachaille Etive Mor, Glencoe, north-west Scotland.
Map Ref: NN 228 546.
Guidebooks: *Scottish Climbs 1 & 2* by Hamish MacInnes, *Glencoe and Glen Etive* by Ken Crocket.
Attitude: Faces east-south-east.
Altitude: 1800ft (548m).
Rock: Igneous, smooth in places but with sharp holds.
Access: Above the A82 Glencoe road, the Buachaille Etive Mor (summit named Stob Dearg) lies at the head of both Glencoe and Glen Etive. (The Kingshouse Hotel and White Corries Ski lift lie well within view.) There are

two well-used approaches: passing Jacksonville or passing Lagangarbh (Creag Dubh and SMC huts respectively). The first is direct, but involves fording the river, the second is gentler and crosses the River Coupall via a bridge. Both meet at the Water Slide.

1. The Jacksonville approach leaves the road at an unmarked car park 3/4 mile west of the Glencoe—Glen Etive road junction (map ref: 236 554) and crosses the river via stepping stones past the black hut of Jacksonville. Then straight up to the Water Slide Slab.

2. The Lagangarbh path leaves the road at Altnafewdh (map ref: 222 564), crosses the bridges, passes two huts and continues straight up towards Coire na Tulaish. Don't go too high, but branch left to contour round to the Water Slide Slab.

To gain the Rannoch Wall from here, continue along the path which starts to rise steeply to an easy rock barrier. Pick your way up this (Moderate in standard), usually on the right, then traverse left to follow a ridge to the left of a wide diagonal gully. (Above lies the East Face of North Buttress, but ignore this as the Rannoch Wall is the last clean wall over to the left.) This ridge leads up under the Rannoch Wall (SE Face), (1¹/₂ hours).

The most striking line is the ramp groove of Agag's Groove (best defined from ¹/₃ height) which can even be spotted from the road. January Jigsaw starts left of this and crosses it at approximately ²/₃ height.

Descent: From the top of the route scramble up the ridges until a traverse (exposed in places) leads left (across a slab, up to a chimney, then across again) to the lower ridge that runs parallel with the face. (Curved Ridge—Moderate). Descend down this to the starting point (polished and crampon scratched) then reverse the approach.

January Jigsaw – Summary

Directly beneath the face and above the gully is a ledge. Start from this ledge at a short pinnacle with a broken top, which is situated mid-way between Agag's Groove and a large detached flake in the gully. (Approximately 30ft (9m), right of large flake.)

1. 60ft (18m). Up the crack for 25ft (8m) until forced left up the natural rock steps to reach a ledge and thread belay.

2. 60ft (18m). Traverse across right to a big flake on the edge. Step onto this and make an awkward move right into a groove. Follow up this until moves up and diagonally right lead to a good ledge and block belays (on Agag's Groove).

3. 55ft (17m). From the top of the block move out horizontally (balancy) right. Continue round into a leaning groove. Straight up this to a niche (possibly belay). Escape by traversing left then up (in about 15ft, 5m) to a hammered-in coach bolt belay. (The Overlapping Crack directly above is Satan's Slit—VS.)

4. 75ft (23m). Move up and step right to pull across into a groove. Continue up this (sloping and desperate if greasy) until moves back left are made onto the wall. (Directly above is the crack of Satan's Slit.) Continue directly up to the top of the buttress or follow an easier groove to the right.

January Jigsaw – Description

Buachaille Etive Mor rises out of the lonely, wild and barren vastness of Rannoch Moor like a super Egyptian pyramid emerging from the flat desert sands. Mighty, yet benevolent, the Great Shepherd of Etive stands alone at the heads of both Glencoe and Glen Etive, spanning the history of Scottish mountaineer-

JANUARY JIGSAW: 250ft (76m).
Very Difficult (Hard).

JANUARY JIGSAW

Satan's Slit

Agog's Groove

John Hargreaves

Sandra

large detached flake

belay point

January

Broken Topped Pinnacle

ing. To describe it solely as beautiful is not enough, for this mountain, with its classically simple and symmetrical form (as viewed from the road), has long been the emotional symbol that means, to the mountaineer, The Scottish Highlands.

As a youngster it was the first mountain I recognised on our annual Scottish holiday. Our mode of transport was the motorbike and sidecar; with dad cranking open the throttle downhill past the Kingshouse, brother on the pillion seat with his eight-foot woolly scarf flying behind and me, on mum's shoulders, head out of the top of the sidecar. As soon as we saw the Buachaille that was it—we were definitely in Scotland. No mean achievement, indidentally, for it was a pre-motorway journey on a 500-cc Ariel Red Hunter.

In practice the Buachaille is a complex of different walls and buttresses and in bad conditions, especially in winter, requires extreme care to descend in safety. I have chosen a route on the Rannoch Wall for this is a magnificat area of rock on which to climb.

Partly this is due to the nature of the blood-red-to-black rock which, although tight and smooth, offers a number of natural lines with regular square holds and the odd good flake. But mainly, it is due to the physical position, for the wall rears up from an already airy stance overlooking Rannoch Moor, catches a fair amount of sunshine and offers a spectacular view. W. H. Murray described the climber on this wall as being akin to a fly crawling on the face of a skyscraper. An evocative and accurate description.

I suppose Agag's Groove is the most famous of the climbs on the wall, (and rightly so for it is the most immediately striking) and I suppose Whortleberry Wall is one of the most satisfying long, protectionless, leads to be had almost anywhere. But January Jigsaw is my choice of route here, quite simply because I found the whole climb to be totally absorbing.

The team was assembled one night in the back bar of the Clachaig Inn. John Hargreaves was keen and enthusiastic, despite the first sleet of winter that was driving through the Glen. This was good, but in order to take the photographs I needed a third member. Sandra, I recognised from a previous trip, solely because she was then on crutches and now was not.

'Walking again?' I enquired.

'Oh Aye,' came the reply.

'You'll be wanting to do a route then,' I joked.

The following morning the three of us set off, amongst the wind and showers, to the Rannoch Wall.

Occasionally the sun would burst forth, resulting in two consequences. One being that brilliantly coloured rainbows would either appear almost encircling our feet, or out across the Rannoch Moor, accentuating the scale of this four-hundred-square-mile wilderness. The

other was that we felt compelled to climb the route.

Even from the first few feet, up the crack behind the little pinnacle, January Jigsaw lets you know it's not going to be a pushover. In the wet and cold, even as third man (second man actually—but third person!) I found the going steep and a bit insecure, sure-placed footwork being the order of the day as the handholds, although consistent are not generous in their nature. The staircase of natural rock steps leading up leftwards should have been easier, but the lack of friction even made this demanding.

A reassuring thread belay on an airy, but reasonable ledge is then taken. From here the position becomes absolutely spectacular as you traverse out to the edge with, seemingly, the whole of Glencoe at your feet. A large flake leans against the wall and you stand on this to make a decidedly awkward move round into a groove. John ran out a lot of rope here, with no further protection, on steep ground and in difficult conditions. It was a good steady lead.

You then land, with good belays, onto Agag's Groove, but it is only after this that the really interesting climbing begins! I think you should discover this for yourself and I will only repeat what the locals said to me—'Och Aye, it's only Very Difficult—but hard if you ken what I mean!'

As we tramped back towards Lagangarbh, sodden but very satisfied, Sandra said:

'I'm seeing the quack tomorrow; he should be pleased. Last time he reckoned I may be able to bend my leg sufficiently to sit down by the time I saw him again!'

'How long have you been off crutches?'

'Three weeks now,' she giggled gleefully.

'WHAT?'

'Grand as a bag of ferrets,' exclaimed John.

Above left: **Sandra White approaching the rock steps on the first pitch.**
Above right: **Traversing delicately out from the block on Agag's Groove, pitch three.**

SCOTLAND: Cioch Direct, Arrow Route, integrity (Combination)

CIOCH DIRECT: 500ft (152m). Severe.
First Ascent: H. Harland, A. P Abraham, 1907.
ARROW ROUTE: 200ft (61m). Severe (mild).
First Ascent: J. Allan, 1944.
INTEGRITY: 250ft (76m). Severe (hard).
First Ascent: D. H. Haworth, I. E. Hughes, 1949.
Location: Cioch face of Sron na Ciche, Black Cuillins, Island of Skye, north-west Scotland.
Map Ref: NG 443 203.
Guidebooks: *Skye* by J. R. MacKenzie (SMC Guide). *Scottish Climbs* (Vol. 2) by Hamish MacInnes.
Attitude: Faces north-north-west.
Altitude: 1800ft (549m)
Rock: Gabbro (often claimed to be the best and roughest rock in Britain).
Access: Skye and Glen Brittle are best reached (by car) travelling along the Skye road from Fort William to the car ferry at Kyle of Lochalsh (operating regularly until 2300 hrs. in summer). The best approach is from the beach car park at the end of Glen Brittle. Take the well trodden path, rising from the campsite, passing Loch an Fhir-Ghallaich until it branches right, finishing up scree, to the base of Sron na Ciche. (This massive NW face is almost 1 mile, 1.6km, long and reaches 1000ft, 305m in height). Continue along the base of the cliff leftwards until a chipped boulder (showing 'CD ↗') and a walled bivouac site beneath an obvious downward pointing fang of rock mark the chimney start of Cioch Direct (1 hour).

(Arrow Route can be gained independently by traversing in from left to right along the 'Terrace'—the large shelf running below the prominent block (or breast) of the Cioch. The terrace starts left of the bottom of Eastern Gully and rises diagonally rightwards across the face crossing through Eastern Gully and continuing on below the Cioch.)

Descent: At the top walk leftwards to the top of Bealach Coire a'Ghrunnda (the pass leading over to Coire a'Ghrunnda). From here descend easily over mixed scree and boulders to regain the base of the cliff and the start of Cioch Direct.

Cioch Direct – Summary

Start at the well defined chimney, giving access to the continuous diagonal line of cracks and grooves leading leftwards to the foot of the Cioch. (Not obvious from below

Looking to Sron na Ciche and the Black Cuillins.

the Cioch is a huge block of rock, situated half-way up the cliff, sticking out proud: hence the name—Cioch means breast.)

1. 130ft (40m). Up the chimney to where it opens out and continue to a good ledge on the left arete.

2. 80ft (24m). Continue up the steepening groove to below the vertical corner.

3. 70ft (21m). Climb the corner to move precariously into the chimney (crux). Squeeze up this until its top and over a block to belay.

4. 80ft (20m). Up the corner for 15ft (5m) to the overhangs then move left to a slab gangway beneath the overhangs. This finishes up a deep rock V-groove. At the top of this there is a thread belay opposite to the large cantilevered rock slab—a little cioch (most obvious from above).

5. 70ft (21m). Traverse left to the corner twin cracks. Up the steep wide crack to gain an exposed but easy slab. Continue up to belay on large ledge.

6. 35ft (11m). Scramble 25ft (8m) left to a rock platform. Thread belay down on left end.

7. 45ft (14m). Up the shallow corner in wall and continue to a very large boulder—strewn ledge below the Cioch ('The Terrace').

Arrow Route – Summary

Continue directly from the ledge.

1. 80ft (20m). Climb easily up and make a long traverse left to belay in a little niche in the very obvious diagonal fault.

2. 120ft (37m). Go straight up (as the name implies) using the naturally scalloped pockets in the slab. From the top-most horizontal/diagonal break move up into a slightly rightward-leaning scoop which leads, delicately, in 20ft (6m) to the sharp edge of the ridge (which runs from the main face to the Cioch). Tumble over this to find a thread belay underneath the wall just to the left.

Integrity – Summary

This lies above and almost directly in the line of Arrow Route. Start by following the chimney/rake left for 20ft (6m) to the first break through the overhangs—a short, steep, scooped chimney.

1. 160ft (49m). Up the chimney to pull steeply into the slab. Follow the crack to the next overhang. Pull steeply through this to follow the unbroken crack which leads, in

Above right: **The whisper of a scoop on Arrow Route. Climber: Duncan Richards.**
Right: **Louise McMahon ending the first long pitch of Integrity.**

CIOCH DIRECT: 500ft (152m). Severe. ARROW ROUTE: 200ft (61m). Severe (Mild). INTEGRITY: 250ft (76m). Severe (Hard).

another 20ft (6m) or so, to a corner ledge belay.

2. 100ft (30m). Continue directly up the corner and up through the steepest section to reach a series of large apparently detached (but sound) blocks. Step left a few feet then continue directly to the top.

Cioch Direct, Arrow Route, Integrity (Combination) – Description

The sight was stunning: in front the moon hung, silvery yellow, symmetrically above the bow-shaped ridge (Bealach a'Gharb-Choire) separating Sgurr Dubh Mor and Sgurr nan Eag. Behind, the last spluttering remnants of a vivid orange fire disappeared into the infinite horizontal blackness of the Atlantic. A world of bare rock of spectacular form and colour, surrounded us: jagged saw-toothed ridges, ragged pyramidal summits, great sweeping cliffs revelled in purple blacks, golden reds and ghostly whites plunging into an all-extinguishing darkness thousands of feet below.

It was the end of an autumn day in the Black Cuillins and Louise McMahon, Duncan Richards and I were standing above the mighty gabbro cliff of Sron na Ciche having just completed a magnificent day's climbing. Our height above the rest of the earth, our solitude, the splendour of the scene and the recent memory of a wonderful day on the rocks, snatched at the last minute from the wettest of summers, all made it into an unforgettable mountain experience.

Our choice of routes, Cioch Direct, Arrow Route and Integrity, took us from the base of the cliff to the very top in, virtually, 1000ft (305m) of consistently excellent climbing. It is an appealing linking of individual routes, one following directly on from the other, giving elegant and varied climbing on what many consider to be the roughest and best rock in Britain. Perhaps the most remarkable feature about this combination of routes is the totally sustained nature of the climb; difficulties come and go but the actual climbing quality does not relent. There are no long broken sections, (patches of vegetation or easy rocks to be merely scrambled upon) for its a 960-ft (293m) long rock climb as near flawless as makes no difference.

Despite all this, individually, each climb retains its own distinct character. Cioch Direct offers a series of steep cracks and chimneys. Arrow Route, so aptly named, takes an uncompromising slab with the crux at the top. Integrity is steep, overhanging in places, and takes a bold line through some very unlikely looking ground. To add that little extra, although many may consider it sufficient motivation in itself, the ground covered gives splendid views of the famous Cioch and convenient access to its 'summit'.

We set off with the gut feeling that it was going to be a great day; the early morning ferry over to Skye had already shown the Cullins like I'd never seen them before, and now there remained hardly a cloud in the clearest of blue skies. Louise promised that a cloud would most certainly appear and park itself over Sron na Ciche but, this is unique in my experience of the Cuillins, not one of us seriously believed it. On up the great bog trot from the sea, past the black-blue waters of Loch an Fhir-Ghallaich, the islands of Soay, Canna, Rhum, Eigg and the Western Isles floated on a resplendently turquoise sea—so clear you felt you could touch them. Then in the distance, looming in the shadows, the grey gabbro of the Sron na Ciche appeared and slowly, the reality of the sheer unbroken height of the crag dawned. A thousand feet high (305m) and nearly a mile in length, it takes a little time to grasp the truth: it is huge.

As you move closer and higher the long grass and the peat vanish completely to leave a scene composed entirely of rock. For the climber to be in such surroundings on a cloudless day is nothing short of a spiritual experience. Here was the answer as to why the rugged mountains of the Black Cuillins have traditionally been the holy shrine of British rock climbing.

Of our destination, Sron na Ciche, it is the western buttress, to the right of the Cioch face, which first draws your attention. Observed from the path, the central section of unbroken slabs shows lighter than the rest and they plunge, unbroken, the full height of the face. It is, however, the lesser-looking Cioch face, partly overlooking the large black Eastern Gully on the left, which offers the more interesting climbing. The gabbro here is more consistent in quality and the intrusion of black basalt, which doesn't offer the same angular holds and is lethally frictionless when wet, is much less frequent. The feature after which the cliff takes its name, the Cioch, is situated some 500ft (152m) above the ground. Not at all obvious from below, its presence was only suspected by Professor N. Collie when he noted its shadow cast on the opposite side of Eastern Gully. But once reached it is spectacular enough, as he discovered.

Directly below the famous feature the line of Cioch Direct slants steeply leftwards, making its way through a gigantic stretch of gabbro—a continuous linking of chimneys, grooves and cracks. This is my kind of line, absolutely obvious and straightforward, a challenge that cannot be ignored. The bottom pitch looks easy enough, but the face is big and, higher up where the vision starts to blur scale and detail, the rock appears to bulge and overhang leaving a question mark as to its feasibility. At this point you're hundreds of feet up, tackling

the easiest line on a large, unbroken section of rock, with no simple escape to the right or to the left. A significant undertaking on the first ascent in 1907 and an irresistible one ever since.

Most often the route will be climbed in the shade, as the sun is reluctant to hurry itself on to these northerly-facing sections of the cliff, and, Skye being Skye, the route will inevitably

Duncan Richards and Louise McMahon on the famous Cioch.

weep a little in places, or you may even choose to do it in the rain. But not to worry; the rough angular nature of the gabbro provides both good positive holds and superb friction and this more than makes up for any slight polishing of the rock.

For those with energy to spare or time on their hands after the climb; the start of the route, a deep little chimney, is flanked on its left side by a sharp dog-tooth downward pointing flake of rock, concave on the chimney side, and offering above the bulge two distinct handholds—an interesting mantleshelf problem. But onto the climbing, for only the blindest of rock athletes would visit the Black Cuillins to boulder.

After two long pitches, providing high exposure, the difficulties begin. Within a few feet, an awkward exit into a chimney is effected with poor handholds and a reasonable degree of commitment. This is thought-provoking enough, probably the crux of the climb, but those with any failing in their chimneying technique will be struggling above; I got positively jammed solid and made upward progress only by prising the crack open with a brutish display of ineptitude! The next pitch is a complete contrast and once the overhangs are reached a tremendously airy traverse is followed leftwards and upwards under the roof. This section could be imagined to be a groove rotated to now offer a ramp for the feet, and occasionally, a roof on which to reassuringly rest the back. A superb heavenly staircase providing the key to moving through the steepest section of the rock.

The belay gained is best viewed from the next pitch, it is a sizeable cantilevered block of rock secured to the cliff by gabbro friction and Skye magic—a miniature Cioch. Good climbing still remains and a corner is followed utilising the twin cracks which lead to spectacularly placed, but easy, slabs leading to a rock ledge. A traverse and a short wall take one up to the Terrace. Above towers the black and mighty Cioch.

We chose the Arrow Route, a line taking the steep, clean, unbroken slab left of the Cioch. Its direction is bold and its situation appealing. On the right the black Cioch rests regally, and below the Eastern Gully adds instant exposure. The first pitch wanders up to a diagonal break and ambles its way over to the left to gain a belay in a sloping niche. A sea of rock hangs above. Only when one makes the effort and moves off directly upwards, is the secret of its possibility made known. The whole wall is scalloped with half pockets just enough, along with the available friction, to make comfortable progress up the wall. Of course, the simple explanation to the presence of these unexpected holds can be clearly understood when one remembers the popular footwear that was traditionally used in the Cuillins, thousands of nailed boots, scraping earnestly at the rock, have formed them so.

Continue, arrow like, straight up the wall until within 20ft (6m) of the top a slightly rightward-leaning whisper of a groove can be delicately gained and followed to the sharp Whaleback ridge that connects the Cioch to the main cliff. I actually placed two nuts in this 120ft (37m) pitch, both offering security where I felt it necessary. Without these, as would be the case up to the 1980s, the whole pitch would have presented a piece of rock climbing where a slip would have been most serious. Today it still requires a carefully controlled and precisely executed sequence of moves to safely make the belay.

Most now find it compulsory to scramble (Moderate) across and up to the top of the Cioch, as we did, but our next route lies just to the left—tackling the head wall virtually directly above the Arrow Route. Integrity is some fantastic rock climb. The ground it covers, a vertical wall teeming with overlaps, looks only practical at a grade considerably harder than Hard Severe. Nevertheless, Hard Severe is a true and realistic grade.

A crack continues for the entire length of the climb and takes you steeply through the initial bulge (the technical crux), on up the wall to surmount a second, difficult overlap, and, with 50-m ropes, to a secure rock belay in a little corner. There is always a good hold right where you want one and, with the steep ground to be contended with, this makes the pitch into an absolute dream. The next pitch rivals the first for steepness and takes you from this huge, now vertical, face of Sron na Ciche out on to a broad boulder-strewn summit. Out on to the tops with views of the sea and the distinct rugged Cuillins all around.

This is where I began my narrative, but the day had still not yet quite ended. As we descended the stars rose in a sky, still blue, and there was only the sound of silence. But as darkness intensified and we dropped further, we heard the slight wind stir the long grass and then the waves crash, rattle and suck on the nearing shore. The moon shone full and strong, casting our shadow complete and distinct. No one spoke, we were enchanted, Skye, the magic isle, had given us her best.

SCOTLAND: Eagle Ridge

EAGLE RIDGE: 670ft (204m). Severe.
First (complete) Ascent: J. H. B. Bell, Miss N. Forsyth, 1941.
Location: Lochnagar, southern Cairngorms, north-east Scotland.
Map Ref: NO 250 855.
Guidebooks: *Climber's Guide to The Cairngorms* (SMC Guide) by A. Fyffe and A. Nisbet. *Scottish Climbs* (Vol. 2) by Hamish MacInnes
Attitude: Faces north-north-east.
Altitude: 3,000ft (914m).
Rock: Granite.
Access: There are various approaches, but the best is from the Spittal of Glen Muick. A sizeable car park is reached at the end of the road—10 miles (16 km) from Ballater. From here

walk through the wood (past Visitor Centre) and turn immediately right. Follow this unsurfaced road to a granite building. (Left there is the Allt-na-giubh-saich Lodge.) From the back of this follow a path (alongside a fence), through a wood, to gain a distinct (unsurfaced) track. Follow this to the Muick/Gelder Col (track widened to Cairn) and branch leftwards on the distinct path. Follow this up to a col (Meikle Pap on the right) and then descend leftwards into the corrie (2 hours).
Descent: Over to the left (looking *out*) is the Black Spout. The main branch (most northerly) of this great gully leads one easily back down to the Corrie floor. To go directly back simply continue along the ridge towards the Meikle Pap and regain the approach path at the Col.

Lochnagar.

Eagle Ridge – Summary

From the left of this grand cirque of cliffs the first huge gully is the Douglas Gibson. The great ridge to the right of this is the line of the climb. Start virtually at the foot of the gully, at the first clean little corner groove just above the toe of the ridge.

1. 100ft (30m). Climb the corner groove and at the top step left into the continuation chimney. Continue up this until a rock ledge and belays are reached on the left.

2. 55ft (17m). Regain the chimney and climb over the jammed blocks to a stance on the face of the buttress.

3. 90ft (27m). Climb up to regain the edge of the ridge. (An impressive position above an obvious red rockfall scar.)

4. 90ft (27m). Move rightwards to a clean corner. Up this and continue to belay on rickety pinnacles on the crest itself. (This pitch marks the opening of the difficulties and the ascent of the ridge proper.)

5. 60ft (18m). Climb the steepening ridge (The Tower) until awkward moves enable a step right. Further steep moves upwards and leftwards lead to a deep cut sentry-box.

6. 45ft (14m). Gain the ridge above the sentry-box and follow this until a short rightward slanting corner enables a ledge and belay to be gained. (Do *not* move off on ledges to the right.)

7. 75ft (23m). Up the short steep wall directly above to gain the ridge on a knife edge. (A distinctive feature viewed from above—known as the Whaleback.) Follow this to a big ledge on the left. Move up again then right to belay in the corner.

8. 40ft (12m). Climb the corner to the crest then make an awkward and exposed move up the wall to gain the next crest. Follow this in a few feet to a corner and stance. (In situ peg belay and No. 1 Friend placement.)

9. 45ft (14m). Steeply up the corner groove then step left beneath a small flat overhang (known as the Coping Stone). Overcome this by swinging up leftwards. Above lies a V-niche which is entered awkwardly, from tottering pinnacles using a horizontal crack handhold high on the left. The groove/niche leads in a few feet to belays.

10. 70ft (21m). Easy rocks lead to the top. (Reasonable time of Ascent—3¹/₂ hours.)

Eagle Ridge – Description

It was only on my fourth visit to the dark Lochnagar that I actually saw the cliffs. Such are the extremes of Cairngorm mountain weather that, although I had climbed them twice in winter and walked below them in summer, I had never actually seen more than fifty consecutive feet of rock at any one time. This fourth occasion was different.

On that day in mid September, with the mountains alive with colour, the purples, greens, browns and golds of the heather and the pinks and whites of the granite, the sun shone in a cloudless blue sky and the wind hardly dared whisper lest it break the silence and perfection of the scene. From the col below the Meikle Pap we witnessed a breathtaking sight. A flash of rich gold crowned a vast blackness as the sun kissed the rocks of the mighty Lochnagar.

EAGLE RIDGE: 670ft (204m). Severe.

EAGLE RIDGE

Douglas Gibson Gully

Eagle Ridge (Initial Groove)

We observed an immense and majestic cirque of cliffs standing high and stretching long across the face of a giant mountain, below which tumbled boulders and scree, falling into the quiet and mysterious Loch. Outstandingly clear, it was a humbling experience; a moment in time that could not easily be forgotten. It was also the day we climbed one of Scotland's finest routes—Eagle Ridge.

The main cliffs lie in a semi-circle above the Lochan which itself is situated at an impressive altitude of 2,575ft (785m) above sea level, with the Eagle Buttress located to the left side. Immediately to its left is the large and forbidding Douglas Gibson Gully, and the knife-edge crest of rock formed by the right wall of this gully and the rocks of the buttress give the classic line of the Eagle Ridge. Sculpted in granite, it reaches a crescendo in its last 300ft (100m) or so where the climb follows the very arete overlooking the vertical rocks that plunge into the Douglas Gibson.

This is a Mountain Severe in every sense of the word. Technically the climb is no soft option and the climb would still warrant a full Severe grade, some think harder, even if it were situated by the roadside. However, it's a minimum of two hours' walk away from the nearest permissible car access point and its remoteness alone makes it an undertaking worthy of some preparation. Couple this with the Cairngorm weather (the possibility of rapid changing conditions from sunshine through driven rain to snow and on to freezing are all possible on almost any day of the year), and one realises the true potential of the climb. If you know these facts and prepare well, the extra effort will be handsomely rewarded, for, as any Cairngorm climber will tell you, there is no better ridge climb in the whole of Scotland.

J. H. B. Bell is one of the greatest of the Scottish pioneers and climbed many new routes throughout Scotland, yet his devotion to this one route was profound. He said, in his *A Progress in Mountaineering'*, 'My enthusiasm for the Eagle Ridge of Lochnagar has the same character of complete satisfaction as the experience of a great work of art.' He, in fact, opened his campaign to climb the route early in June 1936, straightened the line in 1941 and returned again in 1948 to dispense with a point of aid he had previously employed (his second, Miss Nancy Forsyth, had seconded it without use of the piton in 1941).

'There is a region of heart's desire
free for the hand that wills;
land of the shadow and haunted spire,
land of the silvery glacier fire,
land of the cloud and the starry choir,
magical land of hills;

loud with the crying of winds and streams,
thronged with the fancies and fears of dreams.'

(Geoffrey Winthrop Young).

It's only when you get some way up the cliff that it becomes apparent that the rocks of Lochnagar, despite being granite, are sometimes broken and shattered and that there is a wholesome proportion of vegetation. The

John Hargreaves in the initial groove.

angle, too, is somewhat easier than one would first imagine. All in all it makes the cliff more suited for winter climbing than for rock climbing, yet although Eagle Ridge does form a magnificent, and hard, winter route it is also exceptional in that it provides a rock climb of both notable steepness and great character.

We discovered it with only its head touching the sun, the rest was in the shade, its usual

Stepping from the crest and up the awkward wall.

repose. No matter, for the line strikes you even from the Col beneath the Meikle Pap, a challenge that once seen has to be climbed.

The approach across to it follows an indistinct path. This first gains a little shoulder and then ascends steep scree directly to the foot of the Douglas Gibson Gully. Immediately on the right the first chimney groove opens the way to the front of the buttress. This, the continuation chimney and rather broken rocks above can all be rather awkward when wet and seek to hide the true nature of the climb. It isn't long though before the splendid 'raison d'etre' is introduced to you, for at the end of pitch 3 you are beside a knife edge. Here there has been a considerable blockfall leaving a fresh red-pink granite scar sloping off leftwards into the D. G. Gully. Suddenly you feel you're a long way off the ground and that the problems are about to begin in earnest. This indeed is the case.

From now on the granite is much cleaner, the line truer and climbing sharper. Moves rightwards lead to a well-defined corner and this gives steep balance climbing with spaced protection, a pitch well scratched by the winter use of crampons and leading again to the exposed ridge. The belay, on large, flat-topped pinnacles, could well be imagined to be the site of the Eagle's nest. It seems secure, despite the hollow sounds, and gives a comfortable seat on which to admire the magnificent mountain scenery.

Above, the ridge steepens and some strenuous and bold climbing leads to a freakish rock niche, large enough on which to comfortably hide. I think originally this pitch (The Tower) was considered to be the crux, but I personally found two pitches above to be equally hard. The next sections really are on a razor's edge and it's here, more than anywhere else on the route, that the true essence of the climb is experienced: fabulous views all round; tremendous rock scenery and technical interest enough to make you grip hard the fine Cairngorm granite as you view the ridge snaking away below you.

It would be wrong to explicitly detail, blow by blow, the rocks that follow, for essentially the climb is a journey of discovery and the unknown is a vital part of its majesty. Sufficient to say, there are a variety of tough problems to overcome and when easier rocks finally lead to the summit, and the warmth of the sunshine, you will have experienced the joys of a great mountain rock climb. You, too, will have climbed the famous Eagle Ridge of Lochnagar.

'Heard ye the chant? Saw ye the Grail?'

(Geoffrey Winthrop Young).

SCOTLAND: Spartan Slab

SPARTAN SLAB: 755ft (230m). Mild Very
Severe. (3c, 4a, 4b, 4b, 4b, –).
First Ascent: E. P. G. Langmuir, M. J. O'Hara,
J. A. Mallinson, 1954.
Location: Etive Slabs, Beinn Trilleachan, Glen
Etive, north-west Scotland.
Map Ref: 100 447 (OS—Ben Nevis and Glen
Coe).
Guidebooks: *Glen Coe and Glen Etive* by Ken
Crocket, *Scottish Climbs 1* by Hamish Ma-
cInnes.
Attitude: 1400ft (427m). Faces south-east.
Rock: Medium grained, impeccable white gran-
ite. Superb friction.

Access: From the main Tyndrum—Glencoe road
(A82) turn off down Glen Etive near the Kingshouse Hotel. The road ends at the head of Loch
Etive (10 miles, 16 Km). The Etive Slabs can be
seen up on the right, on the flanks of Beinn
Trilleachan. An obvious path veering up the
hillside enables the right-hand end of the Slabsl
to be reached (30 minutes).
Descent: Rightwards (looking in) down the
grass rake above the climbs.

Spartan Slab – Summary

The approach path ends at the large 'Coffin

Above left: **Dave Lyle starting the
slab with the Coffin Stone
behind.**
Above right: **The block overhang on
the third pitch.**

SPARTAN SLAB

descent route

crevasse

peg

base obscured

Coffin Stone (obscured)

belay point

**SPARTAN SLAB: 755ft (230m).
Mild Very Severe (3c, 4a, 4b,
4b, -).**

Stone' directly below the Great Slab. Start 10ft
(3m) left of this below a broken-looking ramp
sandwiched between smooth slabs.

1. 130ft (40m), (3c). Up ribs and grooves to
a peg at 80ft (24m). Step right and go up and
across the Slab to a large soil and grass ledge.
Old peg belay high on left.

2. 100ft (30m), (4a). Step down then up to
gain a crack (nut protection), move delicately
rightwards to follow the obvious weakness via
a stepped groove and up to belay beneath a
rectangular block overhang. Nut and poor tree
belay.

3. 135ft (41m), (4b). Step left (to another
tree) and pull through block overhang, at the
obvious split, to gain crack above. Up this
(entertaining belay may be taken in the
crevasse) and continue up a groove until a
good hand traverse line (invisible from below)
leads rightwards. Up to higher ledge and large
flake belays.

4. 125ft (38m), (4b). Crux pitch, especially if
wet. Go down to horizontal weakness leading
right to another large ledge. (Possible belay on

sharp flake.) Go straight up groove system to
peg runner (visible from belay), at approximately 90ft (27m) (edge of slab lies 6ft (2m) to
right) make an awkward step right through
overlap to gain a crack leading through second
overlap. After a few feet old peg and nut belays
are reached.

5. 145ft (44m), (4b). Continue in the same
line up the narrowing Slab. Assorted old peg
runners (and a few nuts) in corner crack.
Where Slab widens step first right and then
back left and up to gain a large heather ledge
and good tree belay at the end of the Slabs.

6. 120ft (37m). Up the blocky steps just left
of tree until a ledge leads down and
rightwards; eventually to gain the diagonal
grass rake descent path.

Spartan Slab – Description

In the enchantingly beautiful valley of Glen
Etive on the flanks of Beinn Trilleachan, only
half-an-hour's bog trot from the end of the
road, lies the purest, most naked Slab climbing
to be had in Britain. The Etive (Trilleachan)

Slabs appear almost insignificant viewed from the valley, a trick of scale created by their grand surroundings, and it is only on arrival at their foot that the truth becomes obvious. Vertically over 600ft (180m) of white granite sweeps upwards through a series of block overhangs, large enough to trouble the imagination of even the most arrogant of Slab climbers. Horizontal sheets of whiteness span distinct corners which shoot upwards and out of sight.

This large expanse of silver-white granite, broken by the contrasting straight black lines of the corners and linked by the symmetrical curves of the overlaps, presents an organised and unnatural looking three-dimensional structure. Visually the effect is startling and to the diminutive figure stood below, the slabs appear lunar or resemblant of some gigantic space craft.

Without measurement I would guess the average angle of the Slabs to be 45°, rearing here and there to an alarming 50°. Virtually exclusively, progress is made by friction climbing and a cool confident approach is essential for success and safety! Long run-outs, often in excess of 100ft (30m), with little or no protection, require leaders to stretch their necks. Once embarked on a pitch there is no turning back, no escape, for, it is said, 'No one reverses an Etive crux'. There are no bolts here, the pegs are invariably bent and rusting and the very infrequent nuts do not readily bite the tight granite.

In Scottish terms the 'Slabs' are popular; there may be up to five or six parties climbing on a busy weekend. (Weekdays are invariably deserted.) Undoubtedly the quality of climbing is the main reason for this, but there are two other precious features, rare in Scotland, which make it so. Access is quick, being around half-an-hour's leisurely stomp through mud, grit and heather and, secondly, they dry quickly (with the· exception of the corners which can weep black for some time). The drying factor is especially important here because the Slabs become an even more serious proposition in the wet as friction disappears and there have been countless epics generated by parties caught out by sudden rain. Climbs can be done in the wet as witnessed by Allan Austin's and 'Matey' Metcalfe's ascent of Hammer, but they invariably become unpleasantly precarious.

Possibly no longer at the forefront of climbing development, passed-by by the latest activists, the indolent white granite Slabs still

The blind (from below) traverse right on pitch three.

hold their physical power and the legends remain strong. Cunningham, Haston, Marshall, Noon and Smith all left their indelible mark and, inevitably, Whillans too. The latter, where the friction ran out and he began to slide inexorably downwards, turned outwards and ran down the slab—the hard man's way to escape injury! The legacy of the rapid development of the late 50s and early 60s is a host of really great routes and before I detail the particular climb I have selected, to

Pitch four: the crux.

give a feel for the cliff, I think it apt to comment on a few:

On the left, up a great cheese wedge slab (proud of the central area of slabs) is Hammer. A few degrees steeper than the norm, its ascent is made possible by the presence of tiny, but actual, holds.

Going right from Hammer you cross Agony—the great black corner which was once all aid but is now climbed free.

Right, approaching the central area, there lies the Big Ride—aptly named; I've witnessed some incredible falls from this. With the second man belayed in the middle of the White desert the big pitch steps lightly along for about 130ft (40m) with no protection, then becomes hard. The first, I saw, was a Glaswegian who turned onto his hunkers and slid, wildly hollering, at an incredible speed for almost 300ft (100m). Apart from the hole in his trousers nothing was amiss. The second, an English officer, and no doubt a gentleman, rolled and somersaulted in alarming fashion. He was alive, but not good.

Soon comes Swastika distinguished by its nut protection every 90ft, (30m) or so and also by the way it breaks through the curving central overlap, the predominant feature arching over the lower Slabs.

About dead centre starts the technically difficult Pause, a brilliant, brilliant route. Then above the Coffin Stone, situated where the path hits the Slabs, lie Big Wait and Long Reach. I prefer the former, having been lost, hopelessly, on the latter. Both, however, require a distinct lack of imagination as one pads gently, never daring to stop, amongst a sea of granite.

Many Slab devotees will question the route I've singled out from amongst the host of distinguished climbs. As the Creag Dhu would no doubt comment; 'Aye, maybe it's Very Severe, but it's no' fierce.'

Despite this it is interesting, has adequate protection, both in the form of runners and belays; can be climbed quite comfortably when wet, and offers contrasting situations, displaying a variety not always found on granite. On most other British Crags there would be no doubt about the excellence of Spartan Slab. Situated, the easiest climb, alongside a series of bold difficult routes, and being the first obvious weakness to be tackled it tends to be somewhat undervalued by the procrastinating Scot.

Starting a few steps left of the aptly-named 20-ft (6-m) long Coffin Stone, a rather grassy and broken-looking rib breaks the perfection of the enveloping Slabs—this is Spartan Slab. Afterwards the line moves, naturally enough, rightwards and upwards to the right end of the great central arch overlap. On this early section Dave Lyle and myself were climbing in the wet (largely inevitable in the summer of '85). I belayed beneath a waterfall, with the descending torrent becoming airborne at the overlap above my head. It certainly made those balancy steps right into an absorbing pastime, but in all truth with modern rock boots the damp seemed to make little difference—the friction on the minutely rough granite being so good.

After this you move left to a small tree then pull straight through the roof—where a crack has formed due to the overhangs slipping downwards a few feet. Above there is a large fissure and then, incongruously, a deep crevasse. Dave buried himself, rather ashamedly, in here as I had done on my first ascent of the route. But I had an inexperienced second to watch (my excuse for fear).

Some thirteen years before, I suppose, I had found the climb no easier. Hanging around in Glencoe, with no one to climb with, I eventually talked a reluctant father into allowing his thirteen-year-old lad to go climbing. Underneath the 6-ft (2-m) block overhang formed by the arch overlap I was beginning to have a few doubts. If he couldn't do the overhang then retreat would somehow have to be engineered. On that first occasion it was here where the obvious problems began to crystallise; 'He couldn't tie himself on, how's he going to re-belay by himself? The single rope hasn't a hope of reaching the next belay below—but that doesn't matter anyhow he, of course, can't abseil and etc!' Luckily the lad climbed it, often with his sailing pumps being abandoned for his, seemingly more reliable, kneecaps, without undue difficulty.

This was good because up above things looked decidedly improbable. Dave's excuse for not continuing, thoroughly valid, was that he had a good belay and the groove above was oozing wet. That first time I too felt intimidated, all one can see is a steepening groove, leading into the heart of a granite sea.

One must be bold to discover the key, a hand traverse leading off rightwards. A pitch to be remembered. Afterwards moves down and across lead to a ledge (flake belay if required) a few feet left of an edge; a perpendicular break before the next slab system. Above is the technical crux, a groove leading to moves left and then the overhangs which are stepped through with some trepidation.

From the belay, on the edge of nothing, the top of the Slabs hereabouts can be gained in one long superb pitch (150ft, 46m). Delicate friction climbing up a narrow sandwiched slab,

past a number of old pitons, is facilitated by means of layback holds in the corner. After 90ft (27m) one emerges onto the massive head wall of unbroken rock and with little or no protection a feast of balance climbing leads to a resounding tree belay. I found Spartan Slab just as exciting the second time round, but decidedly safer than the first. Better footwear, the odd nut and someone who could belay, countering the disadvantage of the decidedly damp conditions.

Back down at the Coffin Stone, after the perilous grass rake descent had been negotiated, with the untamed and wonderful Scottish hills stretched out before us perfectly framing an unspoilt Glen Etive, I thought, at least in the hills, nothing really changes. The midges proved it conclusively.

The narrowing gangway of the fifth pitch.

OLD MAN OF STOER: 240ft (73m). Very Severe. (4c, 5a, 4a, 4b).

First Ascent: T.W. Patey, B. Robertson, B. Henderson, P. Nunn, 1966.

Location: Old Man (sea stack), Point of Stoer, near Lochinver, north-west Scotland.

Map Ref: NC 017 353.

Guidebooks: *Scottish Climbs 2* by Hamish MacInnes.

Attitude: Separated from mainland by a 30-ft (9-m) sea channel.

Tides: Access at high tides by swimming. Inaccessible in unduly rough seas.

Rock: Torridon sandstone; sound, hard and rough.

Access: Take the road to Stoer from Lochinver and turn off as for Stoerhead Lighthouse. A track goes off just prior to the Lighthouse (leading to an aerial) and this is followed until a path may be picked through the peat bogs. After a mile or so the Stack is reached, just south and west of the actual Point of Stoer (25 minutes).

Descend, easily, the steep grass of the headland immediately opposite the Old Man. The sea-filled channel, must be swum at all but the lowest (when northern end of channel can be crossed in the dry) states of tide. Once across a tyrolean traverse should be fixed for the rest of the party and for retreat.

Descent: On mainland face one full 165ft (50m) abseil can be made from pegs and slings on ledge just below the summit. If only *45m ropes* then *two* abseils are required. First taken to a long ledge (not on route) approximately 60ft (18m) above the base.

Old Man of Stoer (Original Route) – Summary

Start on the landward face by a cluster of pegs and nylon slings (Tyrolean anchor).

1. 70ft (21m) (4c). Move up about 10ft (3m) to traverse the large horizontal crack leftwards (often black and slimy), Friend protection, to reach the large flat corner ledge (possible belay). Pull out leftwards from beneath the overhang to gain a groove, then crack, leading directly up to big ledge.

2. 70ft (21m) (5a). Up the steep wall via a shallow rightward curving crack (crux) to reach overhangs. Climb a crack through these then traverse delicately leftwards to reach good ledge and up again to large thread belay and cave stance. (Large nylon tape in situ in 1985.)

.3. 45ft (14m) (4a). Go right round the corner and follow a high rightward ramp to belay on a tiny ledge (nesting fulmars can be

The lonely Old Man of Stoer.

encountered en route).

4. 55ft (4b). Straight up V groove to ledges (more fulmars) then up short crack or ramp on left to finish.

Old Man of Stoer – Description

Tom Patey, 'Dr. Stack', was the instigator and leading protagonist in the game of sea stack climbing (Old Man of Hoy, Old Man of Stoer, Am Buachaille, The Maiden) and paid with his life when descending from The Maiden, having accomplished its first successful ascent. He's a climbing folk hero; a man with such an aura and charisma that he would draw climbers from, literally, hundreds of miles, just to sit in the same pub and hear him sing and play his accordion, a man with a legacy of wild 'devil-may-care gaiety' unparalleled and a satirist and humorist unequalled in the climbing world.

Times change, heroes and to some extent fun, are becoming increasingly out of fashion in the 'hard' rock climbing scene of the 80s. Athleticism has taken over from talent. A leading rock climber I interviewed told me he had no heroes, no individual whom he unduly respected, his philosophy being that all things are attainable with determination, training, effort etc. All true, I guess, but methinks the climbing world would be a very dull place without its characters and their legacies. Sure, they may subsequently be painted larger than life and, OK, in everyday terms they are humanly fallible, but undoubtedly their characters outshine the colour of their breeches.

To me, athleticism is only a small part of the climbing scene, vital as it is for very hard climbing, for the sport is much richer than one merely involving singular physical activity. Stack climbing is an excellent example of climbing diversity and well displays its other qualities also.

The fact that stacks are merely structured of stone; the result of a now commonly understood geological/physical sequence, hasn't prevented them receiving, through myth and legend, animate status. Each is prefixed 'Old Man' or 'Old Woman' or personified (Am Buachaille means The Herdsman). Somehow the aura remains—a stack has a character and power extending beyond its mere physical form and the climber is the best disposed to discover it.

Hoy's Old Man is the largest and most spectacular stack to be found in Britain and yet the actual climbing quality is not magnificent. Stoer's Old Man is not so spectacular but the quality of climbing is impeccable. The difference is the rock quality; the former is composed of soft red sandstone, an immense (500-ft, 152-m) tottering pile of mostly rotten rock on a hard base, whereas the latter is composed of Torridon Sandstone, (geologi-

Luke Steer finishes the second pitch; Tyrolean rope below.

OLD MAN OF STOER: 240ft (73m). Very Severe (4c, 5a, 4a, 4b).

cally the oldest sandstone in Britain) and has been hardened through the aeons of time. Its composition is more reminiscent of concrete or a superior gritstone and is superb rock to climb on.

OLD MAN OF STOER

abseil slings

nesting fulmars

crux

belay point

It was not too many years after the first ascent that I found myself again greeting the Old Man of Stoer. Passing a solitary peat digger, most likely the same referred to by Patey in his article, we exchanged a few words—'Och you'll be away to climb the Old Man'. We nodded and discussed the stack's origin. 'It's terrible rough out there, you can understand it,' he said. 'There was an Old Woman of Stoer as well, but she was struck by lightning, and that was the end you know. Down there on the cliff a big slab of rock used to lay on the edge. After the big storm it was laid right up over the top. It can be terrible out there you know.' We didn't doubt it (later examination of the site proved there had most probably been a further stack) and with an eye on the ever-blackening sky we hurried towards out meeting with some trepidation.

The Old Man is an incredible, lonely, sight. A thumb of rock standing some 200ft (60m) above a hostile sea, separated from the mainland by a distinct channel of water. He seems to deny any natural laws of equilibrium, for his body expands with height and his head distinctly overhangs his foot. It was rough and gripping and the rock menacingly bleak. I spent an age shaking down the steep grass until finally, truly gripped, a heaving, frothing, bashing grey sea lay dead ahead. Two pairs of eyes burned into mine, 'the lad on the job', and explicit instructions were issued on survival in rough seas. With that, in the first week in May, I found myself swimming across.

Better the second time around when a rather bashful sun, but sun nevertheless, illuminated the Old Man, completely changing his character. The subtle grey-pinks of the Torridon sandstone heightening to reds and blacks as the light flickered between the clouds. The sea was a peaceful green, even on occasions turquoise, and I was no longer 'the lad on the job'.

With hardly any protest, Luke Steer swam the channel and fixed the tyrolean. The 'but I've got to take photographs' ploy working amazingly well. 'Just do that first bit' had him sailing across the horizontal cracks, always slippery and quite hard, and then with a 'just move up with your hands above the overhangs' he was up to the crack and then the stance, all with me clicking away on the mainland.

But then it was my turn. I tensioned the tyrolean rope with a jumar tied off round a boulder and slid across without even getting damp. Luke jeered, I smiled. The traverse I found embarrassingly awkward due to the jams in front of my face being slimy and the footholds, the parallel crack below, suddenly ending. Luke smiled. Moves off the ledge too, I

Above left: **At the end of the
second pitch, the crux wall above.**
Above right: **The crux.**

thought good value, but here the rock loses much of its sea-washed influence and becomes extremely rough, with excellent friction and crisp handholds.

Above curves the crux, elsewhere described as a slab, it could more rationally be called an impending Wall and its ascent is facilitated by use of the curving shallow corner crack on the left. It must be reasonably tricky for Luke paused to place a nut before easily demolishing the rest of the pitch.

After this a huge cave stance is reached where remnants of a TV spectacular adorn the great jammed rock thread. (There seems to be no getting away from TV debris these days.) But soon you will most probably discover another unique facet of sea cliff climbing and the former annoyance will pale into insignificance.

The fulmar nests hereabouts and it required cunning footwork to avoid being puked upon. A few tips may be appreciated; don't lose your cool—it's better being covered in odiously fish-smelling oil than falling to your death. Wait until their eyes swell and their necks bulge then climb rapidly back out of range (up

to 6ft or so). Keep this up until the fulmar runs short of ammunition then move on to the next one (it may be advised to carry a head torch if this procedure is adopted). If the fulmar lies directly above your head close your eyes and pray!

Sandwiched between fulmars is a bottomless groove which is rather awkward and fairly serious—a good belay is essential before tackling it. The ledge above can be liberally splashed with nesting fulmars and care should be taken; if treated respectfully they should give little real cause for concern, before finally the summit is reached.

We descended using two 50-m ropes (doubled) utilising an in situ anchor of various slings and pegs just below the top of the Old Man on the landward side. It's an abseil mostly in space and I, as usual, double checked everything, especially the in situ gear which is so obviously open to salt corrosion. As Patey jibed 'It's a great climb. Three times bigger and better than Napes Needle.' On your way back don't forget to stop and wave farewell, even if it's only two fingers (Patey would have appreciated that) it keeps the Old Man happy.

SCOTLAND: The Mousetrap

Above: **The Dubh Loch.**

Far right: **John Hargreaves tackling the first pitch.**

THE MOUSETRAP: 650ft (198m) Very Sev- (4a, 4c, 4a – –).
First Ascent: J.R. Marshall, R. Marshall, R. Anderson, November 1959.
Location: Right-hand buttress of Creag An Dubh Loch, Southern Cairngorms, north-east Scotland.
Map Ref: NO 233827.
Guidebooks: *Climber's Guide to the Cairngorms* (SMC Guide) by A. Fyffe and A. Nisbet. *Scottish Climbs* (Vol. 2) by Hamish MacInnes.
Attitude: Faces north east.
Altitude: 2,500 ft. (762m).
Rock: Granite.
Access: From the Spittal of Glen Muick. Starting from the car park at the end of the Ballater road (10 miles, 16km from Ballater) walk through the wood (past the Visitor Centre) and continue along until a path leading rightwards

(at the bottom of Loch Muick) crossing to the other (north) side of the Loch (ignore the left fork to Glen Clova). Continue along the Loch, passing the Glas Allt Shiel Lodge (near its end) and continue up to the Dubh Loch. The right-hand Buttress is best reached by continuing along the right side of the Loch, skirting across to the crag at its top (2¹/₂ hours).
Descent: Down the Gully Central, or, if snow filled, move onto the buttress on the right (looking *out)* and continue easily down the crest until it is possible to cut leftwards into the lower section of Central Gully.

Spartan Slab – Description

Viewed from the head of the Loch a deep gully splits the crag. The route climbs the right-hand buttress. Some 150ft (46m) vertically above the toe of the buttress lies an obvious band of black overhangs and about 50ft (15m) left of this lies a cluster of black vertical cracks running up the face to enter a grassy bay (at 200ft, 61m height). These and the continuation cracks above give the line of the climb. A little way left of the actual foot of the buttress a grass ledge gives access to a groove. (Above this grass ledge lies a diagonal crack-seamed slab ending at the cluster of black cracks.)

1. 60ft (18m), (4c). Step right into the (hidden) groove. Where this steepens traverse left across the slab to belay on the small rock ledge below the central system of black cracks.

2. 150ft (46m), (4c). Climb the cracks directly above to reach the grassy bay and continue to the corner at its top left.

3. 150ft (46m), (4a). Step left and climb the steep corner to re-enter the crack system. Climb this to a convenient belay.

4. 150ft (46m). Continue up the cracks.

5. 140ft (43m) (approximately). Broken ground remains to the top.

The Mousetrap – Description

The walk to Dubh Loch is miles and miles long, but it is easy walking and takes only 2¹/₂ hours—well worth the sacrifice for the rock climber who will be greeted by the Cairngorm's largest, most continuous area of unbroken granite. Tight and steep, there are no worthwhile easy routes here; grades start at Very Severe and rise to E6.

Driven south by wet Cairngorm weather, Graeme Livingstone, perpetrator of the Dubh Loch's E6 (Improbability Drive), sat opposite me in the pub.

'Dubh Loch wet?' I asked

'Unlikely,' he retorted and continued, 'you shouldn't believe all you read.' Then he said it dried very quickly and urged me to pay a visit, feeling sure I would benefit from the experience. In truth, whilst the monolithic and relatively blank modern lines dry quickly, it is certainly not the case with the better defined earlier/easier classics which can be dripping for most of the summer. So I replied, 'Aye, perhaps you're right, but I couldn't face the trudge just to be bored to death by those endlessly repetitive granite moves.' He was stunned into silence. A rare occurrence, most probably unique.

In fact, I've ventured to the bold and distant Dubh Loch on a number of occasions, braving the walk to taste its remote offerings. They are rich indeed and combine challenging and technically difficult rock climbing with the idyllic joys of high mountain seclusion and adventure. For a summer evening's bivouac spent amongst the Dubh Loch granite boul-

ders, with the stag's roars echoing around a mirror-calm Lochan, and endless brews drunk whilst laid in the purple heather, it is an incomparably fine experience.

The cliffs of Creag on Dubh Loch form the Lochan side of the 3,275-ft (998-m) high, typically Cairngorm mountain of Broad Cairn. A more than impressive sight, the cliffs range for three-quarters of a mile at around 1,000ft (305m) in height, and the sweep of vertical granite is largely unbroken. The main feature is the great central gully which splits the crag simply into both a left-hand (eastern) and a right-hand (western) buttress, the latter of which can retain the sunshine until midday. Statistically there are over 60 routes of Very Severe and above, including some 37 climbs in the extreme category, but more worthy is the outstanding quality of many of these routes.

The Mousetrap is one of the more obvious lines taking the challenge of the right hand buttress and consisting of a series of vertical cracks shooting upwards just slightly left of the actual toe of the crag. The line was stolen by the Edinburgh raider, Jimmy Marshall, and was appropriately the hardest rock climb in the Cairngorms at that time (1959). It must have been rather a bitter pill for the Aberdonian-based climbers to swallow, especially after Marshall's winter ascent of the fearsomely steep Parallel Gully B on Lochnagar.

The Mousetap was first climbed in November—it was surely during a particularly favourable period of weather, even allowing for the exceptionally high calibre of Jimmy Marshall, for the cluster of crux cracks are very mossy and consequently particularly desperate when wet. These cracks also serve as a natural drainage line and can remain oozing and dripping for months on end. Additionally, snow and frosts can be reasonably expected any time between September and May.

I've been caught in the Mousetrap in early September (twice in fact) starting in blue skies, and then some way up the crux pitch being caught in the pouring rain. Within five minutes waterfalls cascaded from overlaps, and rivers washed the slabs—we baled out; back to our little tent pitched on the yellow sands of the Dubh Loch. A cold night was spent to wake to a scene of ice and frost. Cursing our useless gas stove and numbed fingers, we left despondently. A further occasion in August gave a brilliant two-man bivouac beneath the boulders. We bedded down to a perfect evening, not a cloud in the star-scattered sky, not a trouble in the world. We woke to callous and unremitting rain and yet another forced retreat. Sometimes the walk back down from Dubh Loch along the endless shores of Loch Muick can seem even longer than the approach.

But the climb successfully negotiated is a highly worthwhile way up a very large cliff. The quality of climbing is pleasant enough, serious and difficult if the weather rapidly

THE MOUSETRAP: 650ft (198m).
Very Severe (4a, 4c, 4a, -, -).

MOUSETRAP

2 pitches
to the top

grassy
recess

crux

King Cobra
overhang

Central
Gully

ledge

belay point

es, and it serves to introduce one to the
ive rock topography hereabouts. Ini-
a groove, hidden from out on the left,
n easy access to a curious diagonal slab.
across leftwards and up to a cramped
give a belay below the long crux pitch.
cluster of vertical cracks are climbed
y, for over a hundred feet, until the
the large grassy niche is reached. This is
tion that stopped earlier attempts, they
't find the key to reaching the grassy
It bulges in places with a number of
ard sections, but it is possible to take
able rests throughout. If wet, (often the
it is possible to climb another cleaner
line to the right, although this is
hat harder.
ving up through the bulge on the top
nd side of the grassy recess is again steep
but soon the crack becomes easier and
logically enough, in hundreds more feet,
flat top of the crag. A quick sidle down
gully, admiring the impressive lines of
W Wall, either sees you gearing up for
r climb or pumping the 'old Primas into
. It no longer matters now whether it

rains or shines, for you have the good solid
feeling of your first route on the Dubh Loch
under your belt.

Tom Patey, of course, summed up the
fascination of the Cairngorms best of all and
possibly the last word by the maestro should
be left to him:

'So it's back to the Cairngorms, the Friends
who are true
And the lassies who speak the same language
as you
To hell with the gauloises and garlic and
wine
Its bradies and chips in the old Brauch-
dryne
To the mountains where Smith is a time-
honoured name
And a handshake from Brooker the passport
to fame.
Wherever I wander, my heart it will be
Where the Auiguille des Cairngorms sweep
down to the Dee.'
(One Man's Mountains by Tom Patey)

Above left: **The first pitch.**
Above right: **Climbing right of
normal cracks on pitch two, to
avoid wet rock.**